THE AHUMAN
MANIFESTO

ALSO AVAILABLE AT BLOOMSBURY

Ecosophical Aesthetics: Art, Ethics and Ecology with Guattari, ed. Patricia MacCormack and Colin Gardner

Posthuman Glossary, ed. Rosi Braidotti and Maria Hlavajova

General Ecology: The New Ecological Paradigm, ed. Erich Hörl, with James Burton

Philosophical Posthumanism, Francesca Ferrando

The Last Humanity: A New Ecological Science, François Laruelle (forthcoming)

THE AHUMAN MANIFESTO

Activism for the end of the anthropocene

PATRICIA MACCORMACK

BLOOMSBURY ACADEMIC
LONDON • NEW YORK • OXFORD • NEW DELHI • SYDNEY

BLOOMSBURY ACADEMIC
Bloomsbury Publishing Plc
50 Bedford Square, London, WC1B 3DP, UK
1385 Broadway, New York, NY 10018, USA

BLOOMSBURY, BLOOMSBURY ACADEMIC and the Diana logo are trademarks
of Bloomsbury Publishing Plc

First published in Great Britain 2020

Cover design by Charlotte Daniels
Cover image © Shakzu / Getty Images

A catalogue record for this book is available from the British Library.

A catalog record for this book is available from the Library of Congress.

ISBN: HB: 978-1-3500-8109-3
PB: 978-1-3500-8110-9
ePDF: 978-1-3500-8111-6
eBook: 978-1-3500-8112-3

Typeset by Newgen KnowledgeWorks Pvt. Ltd., Chennai, India
Printed and bound in Great Britain

To find out more about our authors and books visit www.bloomsbury.com
and sign up for our newsletters.

For Circe and Francesco

CONTENTS

ACKNOWLEDGEMENTS

Thank you to Liza Thompson and Frankie Mace at Bloomsbury for encouraging me to write this and agreeing to take such a sympathetic risk. Thank you to the many scholars who live their philosophies. These include, but of course are not limited to, those who have read and helped me with this book, including Colin Gardner (with whom I hope to write much more), Ruth McPhee, Chrysanthi Nigianni, Marietta Radomska, Claire Colebrook, Meredith Jones, David Rodowick, Phil Hine, Christina Oakley-Harrington, renee hoogland, Margrit Shildrick, Nina Lykke, Rosi Braidotti, the Queer Death Studies Network, the Posthumanities Hub and the Animal Catalyst Network. This book celebrates the memory of my dear Jane and Steve Ash, and the support of my beloved Gabriel.

PREFACE

This book is a book which calls for action. Direct, available and immediate action. It is not an academic treatise which seeks to deconstruct contemporary issues with which the earth grapples. It does not search for a balanced, logical, emotionless evaluation of how human exceptionalism is perpetuating destructive impulses. Many academic texts already exist which perform this function, and I refer my readers often in this book to their more even critiques of the relevant areas of posthumanism, environmentalism, animal rights and population issues. This book does not seek such an evaluation. This is a manifesto – I seek here to make manifest an alternate way of writing, reading and 'doing' ahuman work. That is, activating forces that seek not to solve our crises but to, at the very least, uncompromisingly shatter the presuppositions which are the foundations of the logic affiliated with humanism (including posthumanism) so that each expression of life, human and nonhuman, has a greater capacity for expression and liberty, and the earth's multiple environments have a chance at one of many varied alternative presents and futures. In order to dismantle the dominance of the human, I have sought to no longer argue like a human, with other humans. For this reason, the term 'ahuman' refers to an alternate way of writing and reading that will definitely meet with resistance but that involves making ourselves vulnerable, available, accountable and careful in different ways. I ask the reader to be aware of this requirement. Disagreement is expected;

as a manifesto, the claims herein are adamant, extreme, unpalatable, even unthinkable. We are in the midst of manifesti coming from extremes too often enamoured of hate and destruction. This manifesto may seem to hate humans. It does not. It simply seeks different trajectories to the more typical political, academic human versus human arguments. It is a manifesto of doing something right now, individually, collectively, artistically. It is a manifesto of joy. But the joy is for all life, not only ours. It is a manifesto that repudiates hierarchy, that refuses that some human rights should be privileged over others, and that human rights should be privileged over nonhuman. These claims are presumed rather than argued, so the calls to action are presented not as balanced contemplations but as para-academic DIY pleas to activism, small and large. I could have grounded this book within a gap in the academic market. I could have offered a slight tweak to existing arguments about animal rights, ecology, population and earth devastation. As I have already paid that due, politely and in a scholastically respectful way in *Posthuman Ethics* (2012), it would be a waste to repeat or update it. Scholastic musings do not seem enough without action. We must live the life we theorise or desire, even if it seems utopic, deluded or extreme, three expected evaluations of this manifesto. But those evaluations are contingent on the level of investment in human exceptionalism of the reader. Additionally, this manifesto requires a little optimism, something increasingly difficult to muster. As a manifesto, this book chooses the adaptability and specificity of individual and environment for the development of the action, so it does not offer a replacement system per se. It is a book that I call a work of radical compassion. Radical compassion is available to all humans. Radical compassion is as simple as it is difficult – simple because very few demographics of humans would be unable to adopt the practices of compassion offered, difficult because addressing our own privilege as humans can unveil a devastating awareness of what human compulsions have wreaked, with which we are all complicit. This awareness is our unmaking, but it may remake the world. I do not ask the reader to agree with this work of radical compassion, but I do ask that arguments against radical compassion be extended beyond concepts that take as their first presumption human exceptionalism, an idea that is just as extreme, subjective, uncompromising and more detrimental than radical compassion. So perhaps while reading this manifesto of radical compassion, I ask the reader to offer a kind of compassionate reading. What matters is how we can still care for and in this world.

Introduction

The end as affirmation

The end of the anthropocene (which I will deliberately not capitalize) is the opening of the world. We are beyond questions of why, as it is clear the anthropocene benefits very few living systems and relations. Complicity with the anthropocene has slowly diminished through the vital affirmative work that seeks to destroy the order of knowledge which perpetuates its own values through its claims to truth. The arenas of contestation have remained within anthropocentric discourse, which is the most sinister element of the anthropocene's limitations on activism. It makes the whole natural world the *differend*, that nonhuman, nonincluded other who cannot speak or cannot be heard. The death of the anthropocene opens up thousands of voices, trajectories, relations and necessary activisms. I use death here as it will be used in the entire manifesto: both advocating for the deceleration of human life through cessation of reproduction, thus death of humans (though, as will be made clear, with care as we live out the lives we have), and the absolute end of perception that apprehends all living organisms and relations through anthropocentric-signifying systems. Activism has long affirmed that forsaking power within the system which constitutes it is the way to change it, and forsaking our human privilege is a way to forsake the anthropocene in order to affirm the world. Activism towards nonhumans and the cessation of bringing new humans are two suggestions, but circumstance will open up radical possibilities that will make the human unthinkable. We are in an age of small tactics, of minor radicalisations, of thinking of ways beyond and ways out, not for ourselves, but for the world. Unlike other revolutions which usually seek to liberate the 'we' as specific collective groups, the contemporary world is dividing humans into two, an overwhelming and growing anthropocene, and what I term the *ahuman*.

Why manifesto?

This book, like most manifesti, sets out declarations at the intersection of culture, art, politics and ethics which call to action. The ahuman is a concept coined in the 2014 collected anthology *The Animal Catalyst: Toward Ahuman Theory* (MacCormack 2014). As its progenitor *The Animal Catalyst* sought, this manifesto seeks to catalyse and so cannot claim to be anything less accountable than a call to affects. As a manifesto, it will likely date rapidly, and this is an aspiration, because if it does not, then the world we occupy right now has little hope. Not that I am claiming that what this manifesto proposes is the only way, but simply that this work demarcates the key detrimental tendencies of anthropocentric privileging human practice which have to change in order to preserve the world. Many other manifesti are being written right now that do the same but offer different escape routes. Mine are selective suggestions. I have tried not to be deconstructive only. Demarcating the problems always comes with a call to other ways, and I have kept some of these very simple – go vegan, don't breed – while others remain necessarily abstract due to their localized and needs-based call to imagination such as death activism and occultism as artistic political practices. Their abstraction is not meant as alienating as many critique abstract philosophy for doing. Rather, abstraction remains in order for adaptability which is unique and applicable to be invoked, what Fèlix Guattari calls the creation of a finite existential territory – a real, material territory which causes change based on the qualities of that territory and its impulses against its own relationship with power as a unified overarching system – Spinoza's *potestas*. Life, the world and human practice are always in flux, but the homogenous and simultaneously endlessly adaptable blanket of capitalism frustratingly offers up as many of its own resistances as minoritarians attempt. As Franco Berardi, aka Bifo, states, 'The post-bourgeoise capitalist class does not feel responsible for the community and the territory because financial capitalism is totally deterritorialized and has no interest in the future well-being of the community' (2015: 204). Bifo asks of himself in his manifesto-like conclusion to *Heroes*, 'I am looking for an ethical method of withdrawal from the present barbarianism, and at the same time I want to find a way of interpreting the new ethical values that barbarianism is bringing about' (2015: 207). I share these ambitions with Bifo, but we diverge when he asks how can we remain human. My response is we should not want to. The strive for solidarity is consistent in this manifesto and the work of what could be called 'post-communist' (or even post-political) writers of manifesti, which is why this book is so inspired by Guattari. However, in this book, solidarity is first treachery, against our species who has already betrayed the very concept and value of life at its most basic definition. This treachery is what I hope will make *The Ahuman Manifesto* valuable even while I will consistently seem to contradict myself by retaining commitments to queer, feminist, anti-racist and other political alterity movements. There is a tension in capitalism's adaptability that I witness daily among students and peers, friends and on social media, between the strong desire to do and be empathic and there for the other, and an exhaustion at just getting by and being at a basic level of existence. And this is the privileged version of capitalism's affects. Survival is what most organisms on earth struggle with. But the lure of the cultivation of individuality as synonymous with liberty continues this exhaustive tension between self and other(s). Most collectives, while remaining pluralist and adhering to what is now known variously as polyvocal assemblage or Kimberle Crenshaw's theory of intersectionality (2019), retain identity and dividuated liberty as a focus, for a variety of reasons, including direct action leading to direct victories, to needing to liberate oneself in order to create enough room to liberate others. Thus, the vast number of manifesti concern a single expression of identity or a set of goals unified by consistent sought-after changes. The genealogy of this manifesto owes much to these: the inherent anti-capitalism of Karl Marx and Freidrich Engel's *The Communist Manifesto* (2004) and Anselme Bellegarrigue's *The World's First Anarchist Manifesto* (2002); the feminism of Sara Ahmed's *Living a Feminist Life* (2017), Donna Haraway's 'The Cyborg Manifesto' in *Simians, Cyborgs and Women*

(2013) and Valeri Solanas's *S.C.U.M. Manifesto* (2013); the beyond-gender questioning of Paul B. Preciado's *Countersexual Manifesto* (2018); the challenges to language, perception and representation of Hugo Ball's *Flight Out of Time: The Dada Manifesto* (1996) and Andre Breton's *Manifestoes of Surrealism* (1969). These chosen manifesti represent only a tiny amount of what I have considered manifesti in my reading, because many texts are manifesti without claiming to be so, in their demand for action and their remaking of the world through alternate perceptions that are motivations to activism beyond, sometimes in spite of, their textual nature. What the works cited in this text share is their inherent disdain for any kind of bifurcating system where action is separated from criticism, word is separated from material reality and, for the ethic that underlies this book, expression extricated from affect. Human identity and dividuation is persistent in many, if not most, contemporary manifesti, both as a project of futurity (transhumanism, accelerationism, even neo-fascism) and a demand for visibility (minoritarian identity politics). I call for an end to the human both conceptually as exceptionalized and actually as a species. Ultimately, *The Ahuman Manifesto* is a call to activism for the other at the expense of the self, not as a form of martyrdom but because life in this book is understood ecosophically as a natural contract. We humans are simply parts of a thing known as earth.

For many, the idea of the cessation of human existence as an absurd claim prevents any engagement with both its possibility and its validity. This is understood as being the immediate response to *The Ahuman Manifesto*. If the history of philosophy itself has been a somewhat narcissistic but also politically invaluable tool in knowing human subjectivity, where often posthumanism is simply a different perpetuation of humanist egoism, then even the death of human exceptionalism is unthinkable. There is nothing martyr-like about devaluing humanity. Ending the privileging of humanity may for some lead to suicide and for others to antinatalism, but neither is a privation demanding acclaim. The greater effects of human absence are more important than dying for a 'cause', so configuring human absence as martyrdom returns the activism to anthropocentrism. Just as the other is 'sacrificed' for human ends in countless human practices – without consent, without a contract – and thus can only be called a martyr by the perpetrators to ameliorate guilt, a manifesto that calls to action is not asking for martyrs because ahumans are willing and vitalistic parts of the assemblage, each with a singular and unrepeatable capacity to act and activate differently. This manifesto is emphatically optimistic and life-affirming; it simply sees the distribution of the value of life differently to the anthropocentric understanding of the world. This is not an uncommon belief, and just as we see passed ages perpetrate practices whose end seemed unconceivable at the time – human sacrifice, slavery, the denial of women to vote – and other practices whose end seems nigh – the illegality of homosexuality in many countries, the denial of entry for refugees into developed countries, climate change denial – the declarations in this book are what a large and diverse collective of activists see as inevitable. A world where humans did not need to do objectionable and violent things and yet did is how we continue to see the past, while acknowledging we still practice human violence, albeit in different forms. This manifesto shares most of its political aims with what is currently known as antinatalist, abolitionist, atheist veganism, which is a growing collective. But I find inspiration in creativity and imagination that is necessary in thinking the unthinkable, which is why the role of occulture and art also play a part in this manifesto. From an external perspective, antinatalist abolitionism can seem only about reactive or privative forces – not doing. It is far from this, which is why I see it belonging to a manifesto as a summoning to creativity. This political arena finds joy in altering the way we as humans occupy the world, and it is not surprising that it retains connections with environmentalism and other deep ecology movements as well as feminism, anti-racism, queer and minoritarian politics of all kinds. It does not lament, it does not mourn for the demise of the human. It takes on the task that does seem impossible, the end of humans. Shouldn't all manifesti deal with what seems impossible? The intimacy between art and political manifesti evinces the relationship between radical creative thought and political change as a single expression of unthinkability, or incompossibility, or whatever posthuman expression could be used which leaves anthropocentrism behind. All manifesti ask is how to express differently to create different affects which can reverberate across multiple relations so affects are created in order to open *potentia* rather than repeat or close off systems of potestas. Art seeks the same practice. From an anthropocentric point of view, I am speaking of many ends – the end of identity, the end of religion, the end of self-serving political movements, the end of human life, the end of the anthropocentric world – ultimately the end of humans' violent occupation of Earth. As David O'Neill states,

Do we not owe it to our fellow life forms, who are our cousins in DNA, to keep them alive so that they can evolve and thrive? Furthermore, the complex web of life on Earth means that if it becomes disturbed knock-on consequences will inevitably follow, including possibly our own extinction. And all because of our vanity and incompetence. So instead of being very afraid, we should be very ashamed. (2018: 316)

The negative value of the end of anthropocentrism is where the jubilance of the world begins. The everything else that comes at the end of these systems is primarily only really the end of the primacy of one isomorphic functioning mode of knowledge. Difference and proliferation which seethes beneath in a germinal state has the capacity to express when the anthropocentric mode is diminished to one of many ways, historical or majoritarian-hysterical. The great debt this book owes to Spinozan ethics can be simplified through this sentiment. The end of a single imposed 'centrism' which dominates global practices ends one capacity for expression by liberating the joy for all other expressivities, and this is the very joy which Spinoza defines as 'good' ethics, the capacity for a thing to express and not be diminished or destroyed by another's detrimental effects. Of course, joy and pain, good and bad, are ways to describe intensities and cannot be reduced to a binary diachronic system. What I hope to privilege is simply the openings for expression. Because anthropocentrism, even in its adaptability through capitalism, wrangles us in its singular potestas, when multiplicities of expression can be unleashed, they will neither belong to a recognisable syntax or form nor be received with clarity and transparency. As in the experience of creating and experiencing art, this messiness should be celebrated because it is difficult to convert to a source or technology of homogenous power. It demands an openness of reception as much as creation. It encounters us with what

Michel Foucault calls 'Outside', the negation of law, the word and the speaker which opens up the void that is a voluminous everything and wants for nothing. Rethinking language this way happens 'when all of language is undone in the violence of the body and the cry, and when thought, forsaking the wordy interiority of consciousness, becomes a material energy, the suffering of the flesh, the persecuting and rending of the subject itself' (Foucault 1997: 18). The anthropocene has refused to hear the significations clearly evident in the violated body and cry of the oppressed, denied language and, as the differend, the capacity, the openness to affect, to be heard. So, clearly, there is a sense of suffering in forsaking privilege, more so for some than others. But this manifesto acknowledges that such forsaking, far from privation and martyrdom, is a creative experience, negotiating Bifo's fear that 'the adaptation of the brain to the new environment involves enormous suffering, a tempest of violence and madness' (2015: 206–7). Bifo is speaking here both of how semiocapitalism is making our brains evolve in unexpected ways and also the requirement that for resistance and activism we must put ourselves at risk of violence and madness, although the madness of artistry is, to me, preferable than the madness of semiocapitalism's fostering of narcissistic paranoia as an entropic equilibrium. In a similar negation becoming voluminosity, taking Ahmed's feminist manifesto where she describes feminist practice as a killjoy manifesto, what minoritarian manifesti seek when wanting to step away from dominant ideologies is to kill the joy that remains unspoken and defaulted to those with privilege. Ahmed's killjoy is only really killing the joy of the singular potestas-imposing producer of power. That it counts as joy in the Spinozist sense at all is questionable, as it is not openness but rank which produces the joy, and the stasis of the relation underpins the joy – joy in power, not in potential, certainly rarely mutual joy between the expresser and the affected. Again, we return to the question 'For whom?' Life for whom, rights for whom, recognition for whom, joy for whom? Then also this manifesto perpetually uses the term 'we'. So when we ask, 'Who is this we?', we are asking, 'How are we as humans affecting the earth?', because whether or not the reader wants to be in this manifesto's 'we', we are all complicit in our own capacities, so while I may seem to homogenize by using the term 'we' against the consent of the reader, tactically 'we' refers to the human, because no human, no matter how post- or ahuman, is entirely without human affects. Thinking of a manifesto as an encounter outside values the constituting space between, the interiority of exteriority, and these forms of activism are jubilant, but they do also hurt because they are hard. It is better, perhaps, to describe the end of anthropocentrism as a form of secular ecstasy than martyrdom. A painful joy where limits and demarcations are dubious and tactical, and aims are towards openings rather than resolutions. A call to action with no end in sight.

A call to

forsake human privilege;

practice abolitionist veganism;

cease reproduction of humans;

develop experimental modes of expression beyond anthropocentric signifying systems of representation and recognition and

care for this world at this time until we are gone.

From posthuman to ahuman

The posthuman after the announcement of the age of the anthropocene seems to have exhausted itself. Issues of transhumanism and nihilism have caused a posthuman despair and world issues a helpless fatigue. More contemporary posthumanism has picked up a vitalistic turn which attempts to reinvigorate a positive end to anthropocentrism. This manifesto traces the development of the impetus to think and live ourselves as ahuman – forsaking human privilege through acts of ethical affirmation that open the world to the other and to difference without forsaking what the posthuman gave away – truth in experience, reality, materiality and life itself. Through practices that acknowledge our human and posthuman history and devastation while devising new modes of action that take us away from human dominating actions, the ahuman proscribes no new template and fetishizes no other in its transformativity. Rather, the ahuman celebrates and demands imagination and creativity in an increasingly impossible world.

In the currently announced age of the anthropocene, demarcated from the 1950s (or 1780s depending who we read), named by Paul Crutzen in 2002 and ratified in 2014, we see an ambivalent attitude that mirrors our biotech political age of the posthuman and extends the age of enlightenment, namely the almost smug position of the human as continuing its perceived location at the zenith of the tree of life, ambivalent even though this hubris comes coupled with a knowing attitude of dread. A 'What have we done?' The tree of life is more a pyramid, and we are the architects of the pyramid and have made all other life, from individual organisms to life systems, the entombed corpses within this pyramid sepulchre. The structures, both of perception and affect, are ours, and the worst tendency in our hubris is the perpetuation of the anthropocene as a result of anthropocentrism, that inability to perceive otherwise than human. A variety of rethink attempts have been made: less and more effective, less and more deluded, less and more detrimental to the nonhuman or what Gilles Deleuze and Guattari call the non-dominant minoritarian, the not-necessarily minority but that which has less access to power and whose only hope to symmetry with the dominant is through a masquerade emulating the dominant. Ironically, the dominant are often most guilty of co-opting and fetishizing the oppressed or the other in their experiments outside of human dominance. Performativity in posthumanism, transhumanism, art and biosciences have turned towards the other, especially the nonhuman other, not towards a becoming-open but rather to their use value as commodities which belong, like the Earth, to the anthropocene. Transhuman technology, mirroring its mainstream counterpart of modern medicine obsessed with life extension at the peril of living quality, has plundered all kinds of nonhuman animals and ecosystems and decimated their right to be by converting their existence into objects of work. Posthuman science–philosophy performs similarly by perpetuating the they/we (more usually 'I') dichotomy by revelling in the idea that humans are collective assemblages of bacteria. While I adore the idea that humans are somnambulistic entities animated by incomprehensibly other life forms, this is another example, like insect collectives and becoming-animal, of utilizing the other through converting it into an apprehensible anthropocentrized ideation. Humans do not create symbiosis. Humans do not reciprocate. Humans use; whether in theory or practice, it all comes down to both being indivisible, because use of any kind directly impacts through its affective expression of an other, on that other's potential to express itself in its own way, whether it is a they or any other form of organism*ing* beyond the anthropocentric form. As Michel Serres would claim, there is nothing natural in this relation. All is a social contract because the interactions are non-consensual, whether we are speaking of human minoritarians or the unknowable other of different species. The posthuman has shown an insipid incapability of the tremendous grace in not knowing and in leaving be. Reverting perpetually to binary and isomorphic indices, the posthuman remains in the realm of action as imposition against passivity as active grace. It both enacts action as a continuation of the humanist compulsion to demarcate and nomenclature, imprisoning the other through the place it gives the other in the subjectified and stratified sphere of life (the inside of the pyramid tomb) and materializes action by repudiating the materialization of the other on the other's own terms. Use, knowledge and comparative equivalence, which is always the foundation of relation with the other, are techniques that have not changed since anthropocentrism. Any deferral from need to want is simply a historical mythologization to vindicate our dominating tendencies. Humans now find ourselves in the difficult situation of knowing what we are doing and why it is literally murdering the earth, but we do not know how to get out of this scenario. There are many reasons, of course, for this impasse, and many are highly contemporary reasons, especially the atrophy capitalism compels in the face of the lure of immediate pay-offs and the almost impossibility of thinking revolution.

The ahuman sees posthumanism in a parabolic configuration to challenge both the evolutionary monodirectional linearity of cyber biotechnic-based posthumanism and the increasing use of nonhuman animals in posthumanism as a devolutionary metaphor. The ahuman's parabola has in one direction nonhuman animals and in the other something which refuses the privilege and signifying systems of the human, but it does not institute a new version of posthumanism which would continue those tendencies albeit in a mutated form. The apex of the parabola is the (now defunct myth of the) human. The nonhuman animal and the ahuman are thus close in proximity but absolutely extricated from each other simultaneously. Ahuman theory comes from two motives. The first is the increasing movement from animal rights (AR) to absolute abolition. AR traditionally serves the interests of nonhumans based on equivalences with humans and is a flawed politics of equality (equal to the human) rather than difference. Abolition sees the rights of any entity based on not what it is but that it is. Human compulsions to define AR define the animal, and the discourse is ultimately one between humans and their dominant perceptions of nonhuman entities in order to vindicate their exploitation of those entities. So all animal studies is inherently human studies between humans of the other and has no nonhuman benefit except in its capacity to catalyse humans to stop being human. In AR and animal studies, the nonhuman is imposed within a structure for which it has neither given consent nor has the power of address and for this reason becomes the differend after Jean Françoise Lyotard's description of the victim who cannot be plaintiff because they cannot manipulate the master's discourse. Abolitionists are activists against all use of animals acknowledging that communication is fatally human so we can never know modes of nonhuman communication, and to do so is both hubris and materially detrimental to nonhumans. Abolitionists advocate the end of all use of all animals for all purposes and select words to exchange for those in circulation in describing the oppression of nonhumans – 'food' (murder and cannibalism for meat, rape and theft and murder of young for dairy and poultry use), 'entertainment' (enslavement), 'research' (torture) and so forth. Abolitionist philosophers are also against the fetishization of nonhumans in posthuman becomings and refuse the use of human perceptions of nonhuman systems and entities because they are assimilative and co-optive. In both incarnations, abolitionism remains antagonistic to, and is considered radical by, AR, animal studies and ethology in its refusal to utilize animals. Abolition, after Serres, follows the tenets of symbiosis, which is a form of necessary care and grace which is a leaving (to) be in reference to human–nonhuman inevitable interaction – a natural contract which overthrows the entirely social contract within which most current debates around nonhuman entities occurs and which thus will always exclude them. The natural abolishes Rousseau's social contract as inherently anthropocentric no matter what topic or object with which it deals. The second motive for ahuman theory negotiates the question of what becomes of the human when it is neither posthuman cyborg nor animal fetishist. We remain non-nonhuman animals, yet we must still acknowledge and account for our biological organism's place within the ecosophical series of relations. Ahuman theory promotes catalysing becoming-other from the majoritarian or all human privilege and renouncing the benefits of the anthropocene. This can occur in infinite ways. Some of the suggestions offered include the use of all manifestations of art to form new terrains of apprehension of the world and encourage new ethical relations between entities, the cessation of reproduction towards the end of the human as a parasitic detrimental species, and thinking differently about death by advocating for suicide, euthanasia, antinatalism and a good life/care of the living over biotechnologies drive for immortality. However, these are few of any variety of tactics which could shift human signifying systems towards ahuman asemiotic reterritorializations of connectivity and novel participations.

Human privilege is yet to be seriously addressed beyond being considered a 'problem'. In a somewhat surprisingly depressing turn, the few vitalist abolitionist feminists, especially Claire Colebrook and myself, who advocate the end of human exceptionalism and are curious about the potentials for openings of life which could become available through activisms such as abolition and human depopulation towards extinction, are aligned with the nihilistic (by which I mean the meaninglessness of human life makes all earth life meaningless through comparative measure) and all male hysteria found in object-oriented ontology and speculative ecology (e.g. Morton 2013). Abolitionist antinatalist feminism is the exact opposite though. Extinction laments loss and meaninglessness laments ever having been but the fear of human extinction is a necessary part of empathy that dismantles human privilege. As Colebrook states, 'Once humans think of themselves as a life form, and then as a life form with the exceptional capacity of thinking or reason, it becomes possible that the potentiality for thinking could cease to be, *and* that such a non-being of thinking is what must be averted at all costs … Yet it is just this sense of entitlement and right to life that might be fruitfully vanquished in an inhuman future' (2018: 150). Colebrook uses 'inhuman' here in an ahuman sense rather than an immaterial or detached sense – a future beyond human privilege. The turn to nihilism is annexed directly upon this exceptionalism, because in the face of an other, be it a cosmic infinite other (with its associations of a new cosmic pantheon, thus, its reminiscence of a medieval early Christian Manichaeism) or a diminutive vulnerable other, the us/ them division is prioritized and the perception always comes from the human, whether in dominance or despair. Yet often when attempts to dismantle the division occur, the human privilege remains, seen in the less obvious forms of human exceptionalist anthropocentrism that attempt to navigate human animal relations, in the field known as animal studies. These sadly remain monodirectional and ultimately parasitic – speaking for and of the nonhuman other is no different to speaking for and as the human minoritarian other, except there will never be any space for consent or a truly reciprocal dialogue even negotiatively. Awareness of the inability of anthropocentrism to open to the other is an implicit part of becoming-ahuman. It is lamentable, it sounds like the task of posthuman ethics is impossible, but embracing rather than lamenting impossible situations is what ahuman revolutions are about. However, there is a difference in the ahuman and the works of Colebrook and myself with many other feminists. Feminism is currently under a difficult obligation, one from which we can learn but potentially also one which we must unlearn. This involves the status of the subject or, more popularly, identity. Like all worthy issues with which the ahuman needs to grapple, the issue of identity presents the activist philosopher with an impossible yet necessary (what Lyotard would call incompossible) task. And it is not a new one, but it does change with time. That is the task of what I see as the need to undo human exceptionalism's major tactic of raising and catatonizing and/or canonizing privilege through the reification of one's identity, which becomes indivisible with one's worthiness. Contemporary activism's intersection with philosophy struggles with the need to dispel subjectivity and its hierarchical power implications while being understandably reluctant to deny the desire for recognition that minoritarian identities seek in direct action especially if one speaks from a position of privilege. Identity is a particularly human anthropocentric obsession, not simply identifying ourselves and other humans but also the act of identifying nonhuman others, objects and relations within an anthropocentric, relatively consistent ontological grid. The act of claiming knowledge is a form of particularly anthropocentric violence in the way that it both proclaims self/and or other from a particularly human perspective presented as neutral and universal, and the way that knowledge affects the known through signifying value, use, closing off potentia (force) in the service of potestas (power), two central forces in Spinoza's ethics of affectivity and expression. Serres states, 'What is conflict? Violence plus some contract' (Serres 2002: 14). Minoritarians have long fought for recognition and for access to those things which form basic perceived rights; this seems the default and obvious choice of activism for those devalued by their bodily demarcations of difference to covet. But as Luce Irigaray has shown repetitively, equality never attends to difference but only demands inclusion through mimesis and assimilation so that included others are lesser but passable mimics of the dominant. The reverse is also apparent, in what Morton has called ecomimesis, where ecologists attempting to reclaim and 'save' nature seek to dissolve the distinction. Never giving up their human exceptionalism ends up seeing this as an empty activity of romanticism and mirrors patriarchy's pedestalization of women (2010: 5, 135). In anthropocentric thought, true difference is not simply a myth but inconceivable because what cannot be conceived via comparison with the dominant remains precisely that – inconceivable. The affects, expressions and forces of the inconceivable need different modes of address towards the dominant, or they risk being reduced to shadow versions accepting and negotiating within the paradigms that disallow difference to emerge. Irigaray in a beautifully anti-identity and anti-humanist turn states,

> A human must give itself a being with faithfulness to the living that it is. In a way it must create its human being through relating to the world and to other(s) – be they plants, animals or humans – thus a being in relation which requires us not to be what they are while being able to be in relation to and with what they are, that is, taking on the negative that the difference represents. (2017: vi–vii)

Difference remains a blind spot in identity based on comparability or resonance, and this blindness is dismissed as a negative or non-being rather than a darkness for non-visual exploration. What can be known is known and evaluated. Difference usually converts in this schema to a failure or lack to be entirely resonant. Identity politics and the activisms of recognition fight for the blind spot of difference to become visible, on the terms of the minoritarian. The inevitable conversion into dominant language this requires in order to be made judicially viable within the social contract is fated to fail difference for this very reason. Ultimately, humanism demands that difference itself must be made anthropocentric in order to count, and for that it is sacrificed to the violence of knowledge and its subsequent significations of value, use and comparability. Minoritarians technically fulfil their status as what Carol J. Adams has termed the absent referent until they make their identities visible enough to be known as subjects over objects. I say technically because human minoritarians in many instances have a greater chance of becoming subject referents through their ability to navigate the anthropocene, the discursive version of what Adams would call the arrogant eye, as the single homogenous lens through which all life and living is apprehended and converted into an index in the social contract. This arrogant eye is the weapon of war, the systematization and normalization of violence. Adams points out this anthropocentric form of knowledge as violence resonates between science (Darwin), holocausts (Nazi Germany, Rwanda), religion (the hierarchy between heaven and earth), so the ideology of the system may differ but the structure itself does not (2014: 19–21). It brings ahuman and other deep ecology theories to a problem that divides us from some of the most influential feminist and radical thinkers of race, sexuality and ability. Recognition is a dissymmetrical form of violence because it is demanded by difference but is contracted on the terms of the dominant. Difference is then diluted and negotiated. The conflict comes from the violence of recognition with the enforcement of a contract written in entirely anthropocentric judiciary terms. Serres states,

> In other words, scientific knowledge results from the passage that changes a cause into a thing and a thing into a cause, that makes a fact become a law, de facto become de jure ... Consequently,

the relation of law to fact, of contract to world, which we noted in dialogue, rivalry, and conflicts, renews itself unchanged in scientific knowledge: by definition and in its real functioning, science is an ongoing relation between the contract uniting scientists and the world of things. And this relation between convention and fact, unique in human history … has not been given a judicial name. It is as if the verdicts of humans coincide with those of objects. This never happens except in miracles and sciences. (2002: 22)

The recognition of minoritarian human identities which has formed some of the most important ethical work in both activism and philosophy is also an advocation in kind of the judiciary nature of the anthropocene, and this is the impossible necessary issue which some of us, particularly Western, usually white, with access to education, have the luxury to explore, while others work only towards personal recognition and most remain voiceless. Here, of course, comes a criticism which is based on the luxury of which I speak. Yes, I am an anti-racist, pro-queer, anti-ableist feminist while also wanting to rid the world of human subjective schemas altogether in favour of the individuation of life based not on groups, tribes, nations, genders, races and species, while actively critiquing any fetishization of alterity so beloved of much posthuman theory. I also seek to navigate the unjustified claim that Continental philosophy and posthuman feminism ignores some humans in preferring non-reified becomings over subjectivity and identity politics. But increasingly humans who fight against humans for the nonhuman other, be they nonhuman animals or environments, are relegated to the status of enemies or, as I have been called, 'traitor to my species'. The idea that we need to privilege humans first then get our Earth into order is a perpetuation of anthropocentric exceptionalism. The idea that an endless encyclopaedia of human subjects must have their human rights fulfilled before the lesser organisms – the very moment where subjects are converted by judicial anthropocentrism to objects – is one of the most nihilistic elements of alterity politics – finding meaning in the meaninglessness of simply being a recognizable identity – because it locates freedom through identity where identity is a grave; it is the moment the flow of life is quickened to a catatonic subject that, no matter how diverse and unique, will still be an object to the arrogant anthropocentric eye. This is why Adams's critiques are so important for an ahuman manifesto. Adams both refuses the arbitrary demand for a choice between humans and nonhuman animals and identifies this demand as what she calls a war on compassion itself. For Adams, care is frightening because it opens the world to encounters through relationality that, in a Spinozist turn, makes us aware of our own effects and compassionate towards the most diverse and minute expressions of the other independent of species, value or perception:

> If feelings were not objectified, we might have developed the ability to interact with the fear, to respect it and the being who is causing it, rather than try to destroy both the feeling and the being. The war on compassion has caused many people to think that it is futile to care. They are unable, imaginatively, to see how their caring will change anything. They experience a passivity inculcated by current political situations as well as by the media. They lack the imagination not to believe that something terrible might be done, but that the something terrible that is happening can be undone.

The war on compassion, further, has caused people to fear that beginning to care about what happens to animals will destroy them because the knowledge is so overwhelming. They prefer not to care rather than to face the fragility, at the least, or the annihilation of the caring self, at the most extreme, that they suspect arises from caring. But caring does not make people more fragile or annihilate them. In fact, through caring, individuals not only acquire new experiences and skills that accompany these experiences, but also discover that they are part of a network that can sustain them even when caring evolves into grief for what is happening. Finally, the war on compassion has caused people to believe that they have to help humans first. (2014: 25)

Some provisos to this advocation of care should be remembered. We are working beyond Cartesian dualism so care of the other does not deny the other agency but acknowledges the power expressions of the self and accounts for our actions. The other is left in independent liberty, which is why Serres's work on the power of grace as a leaving alone is such a powerful example of active passivity as an activism of care. Leaving alone does not ignore or deny the need for care, but it crucially never imposes anthropocentrism on the non-consenting other of nature. It attends and listens, it hosts and gives, it is *careful*. Adams also beautifully elucidates another binary collapse. Here, she emphasizes the logic of care, the design of emotion so usually aligned with women and hysteria that seeks to tackle a frightening, overwhelming need for justice. This logic of care flies in the face of capitalism that asks, What use? It flies in the face of identity politics that says me first or even me too. It flies in the face of any hermeneutic subject when confronted with the 'I am able to do, so *how* shall I do', thus investing all humans, no matter their status or their designation within subjectivity and significance, with action and force, and, by default, accountability and care.

Anthropocentric nature and the ahuman natural

Being belongs to the world of things, where being a subject is being one, albeit the most important, kind of thing, in a world populated by other things, systematically indexed and mapped out in orders of belonging and capacities of similarities and differences. Being and things belong to a way of mapping the world based on force not as vulnerable curious desire – potentia – but as imposed power – potestas. Potestas always precedes the emergence of the life it wrangles into its system, and it always has the maintenance of the system as the primary goal of knowledge. It is knowledge with a motive, or knowledge as motive, differentiating it from curiosity, thought or understanding which extends relations. It is knowledge based on comparison over difference and stasis over transformation of relations where placement of something's being (as thing or being) is as important as any qualities of a thing's being. This technique of apprehending the world belongs to the human. It also extricates the human from the rest of nature while concurrently allowing the human to territorialize all of nature with its assimilative technique of apprehension. When Spinoza states that the foundation of acting ethically begin with will and understanding, he is referring to potentia, will as a force of desire to enter into a relation with difference and understanding as the sought outcome which would see different elements (as collectives of intensities, not 'beings') forming affirmative creativity for both elements as a result of their interaction, whether it be inevitable or sought – what Spinoza calls common notions, commonality without recognition of the other or the commonality itself, just joy. Elaborating Spinoza's definition of commonality as pure capacity to express and be affected, Deleuze states,

> In short a common notion is the representation of a composition between two or more bodies, and a unity of this composition … For when we encounter a body that agrees with ours we experience an affect or feeling of joy-passion, although we do not adequately know what it has in common with us. (1988: 55, 56)

Two beings defined by their beingness cannot enter such a relation. In human discourse, one being's thingness will usually be privileged over another (especially if the other is more 'thing' than being) and its potestas will envelop the other and diminish its capacity to exist freely. If ethics is will and understanding, then humanism is power and knowledge. Will and understanding have no motive for the maintenance of a system. Will understood as desire precedes established systems because 'desire is everything that exists *before* the opposition of subject and object, *before* representation and production. It's everything whereby the world and its affects constitute us outside of ourselves in spite of ourselves' (Guattari 1996: 46, original emphasis). Before human system and structure there is nothing and thus literally everything. The teeming flow of all things within nature as interactive and collective within themselves while being a unity on earth manifests ethics as a hoped for but unpredictable capacity to interact beneficially within and as these flows, to attempt to decrease the diminishment or redirection of other flows if that may be detrimental, to increase them if pleasurable to the other elements. Life and death belong with these flows, as the capacity for negation or affirmation (sometimes both at once). The natural understanding of the world understands the world is formed of chaotic flows. It does not claim to know anything, as to know performs the primary division and enacts the goal of irrefutably marrying knowledge with power, life with being and being with the power to know. The word 'nature' comes to mean nature according to human knowledge, and so there is nothing natural about any claim to what happens in nature: 'philosophers call natural law a collection of rules said to exist outside of any formulation; being universal this law would follow from human nature. The source of man-made laws, natural law follows from reason inasmuch as reason governs all men. Nature is reduced to human nature, which is reduced to either history or reason. The world has disappeared' (Serres 1995: 35). Beings are all human beings in nature because they are defined by humans and afforded their qualities, which directly correlate with their rights to freedom (usually to their detriment). Nature is a knowledge, the natural is a series of relations. Humans exist as occupants of nature, but the lives of what humans call beings also exist within the natural. Life and death occur in anthro-nature as indices of events and records of occupants, which makes nonhuman and human genocide ordinary, while single human being death is lamented. Affirmation and negation occur in nature only as what counts and what doesn't, a binary system of recognition through verisimilitude with the human being or a refusal to acknowledge an other who exists always as an equal within natural relations but may not within human knowledge of nature. Affirmation and negation are quantitative only within a human system. In the natural system, affirmation and negation are qualitative ethical measures correlative with will and understanding, and life and death are occurrences between relations as much as of individual elements. In the natural system, elements understand that their relations may cause the life and death of other elements through their expressions and the affects upon other elements. In human discourse, knowledge provides a 'reason' for death if it is for a lesser being or thing and thus vindicates the human of responsibility for that death or makes death a social issue to rally against, confirming the outrage of the possibility at the negation of 'the human' against all other life. And, most importantly, the human decree of natural law states humans are always the bearers of this law, its justice and execution.

Problems with potestas

To know is already to have negated. Control, according to Guattari, involves three series of subjectification. This already emphasizes that in order to be known, one must be recognized as a subject, and if one cannot be known, one is neither subject nor recognizable. These series are paths/voices of *power* via external control of minds and bodies, paths/voices of *knowledge* through technoscientific and economic articulations and paths/voices of *self-reference* where the self-consistent subject creates relations with mental and social stratifications (1996: 114). We see here there is no 'outside'. However,

Guattari finds most hope in the third voice, the self-referential voice, because it offers the most malleability or opportunity for traversal from power and knowledge. The inextricability of power and knowledge elucidates that knowing something has no relation with encountering it, entering into a relation of expression and affect with it, but, rather, subsumes and assimilates it into finite possibilities of experiencing it before it arrives. When Spinoza states 'Nature has no particular goal in view, and final causes are mere human figments' (1957: 174–5), knowledge describes the goal before the event which would develop the cause (relation) and goal (known subject/object). Spinoza is adamant that interactions cannot be predicted in the future in ethical relations, and nowness trumps future expectation in encounters (1957: 117–19). Indeed, Spinoza associates the predictive attitude to belief in good and evil and superstition in general (1957: 118). Predicting future relations necessitates predicting both self and other as known. From a Spinozist perspective, the claim to know self or other in the future negates both the value of immanent relations of being in the present and relies on a kind of superstition above and beyond immanent relations that gives action a motive rather than the desire for an ethical encounter, which raises or diminishes self and other. It privileges self and other over the relation, which is what should constitute the self and other at the site of the encounter rather than the relation being defined by preceding (and presumed succeeding) qualities. Knowledge and power come from above, and structure encounters via potestas even while they are internally navigated by human subjects. Ethical encounters navigate each entities' thingness as potentia through the relation alone, and so neither can be known in advance. Taking this to an activist practice, Guattari finds in the third path/voice 'creative, transforming, self-reference, in relation to the first two, modes of power and modes of knowledge' (1996: 115). Activism within an anthropocentric framework is, for better or worse, individualistic. Self-referential navigation of power and the concept or possibility of knowledge itself creates activism, because it first involves an active unknowing of what is presumed to be true because it is common. In this sense, to claim to know something is already to negate the unique expressivity of its force in favour of the power enforced by the structure of knowledge upon the self. Unknowing, or the death of knowledge, is affirmative.

> I have said both that self-reference is the most singular, the most contingent path/voice, the one that anchors human realities in finitude, and that is the most universal one, the one that effects the most dazzling crossings between heterogeneous domains ... It is not so much this path/voice is 'universal' in the strict sense, but that it is the richest in what may be called *universes of virtuality*.
> (Guattari 1996: 115, original emphasis)

If knowing is negating, and knowing comes from the homogenous domains of power and knowledge whose individual epistemes reiterate each other in order to create consistent values across seemingly disparate fields, then activism must creatively unknow. Guattari's emphasis on finitude mirrors Spinoza's on the newness of ethics, as activism cannot think strategically but must think materially and actually.

For abolition, the idea of knowing as negation is much more clear. Claims to know animals and what they deserve and what their rights should be are founded on the social contract which repudiates the natural order and places humans at the apex of existence. Any knowledge, all knowledge, whatever it is 'about', is human knowledge and serves human interest via the first two pathways. Human knowledge negates the nonhuman other (and oftentimes the minoritarian human other). The logic of science is also the vindication of humans sacrificing nonhuman others. Knowledge converts the fact there is no need for these acts of murder into a phenomenon of reason over ethical encounter.

> But if suddenly the sciences, which benefit from the aura of sacrificial victims and from the justified triumph of their own type of reason in the time of history and the space of the whole Earth – if the sciences were to take over by becoming, in turn, a total social fact, and dictating their truths to ethics, to laws, to politics, to religions, to philosophies, then injustice would return. (Serres 2002: 79)

Serres shows all claims to knowledge, be their episteme valued more or less, risk becoming unethical systems of potestas which negate the other and close off paths of virtuality.

Reason is not will/desire: While often being utilized in traditional AR arguments (somewhat ironically considering that utilitarian AR arguments argue for compassion for animals because we are intellectually 'superior'), reason has a troubled relationship with minoritarian activisms. Irigaray defines sharing of speech – a conduit to love – as 'no more simple mastery of the self, of the objects of the world, even supposing some respect, but a letting be that does not impose an already existing language as a guardian to life and growth' (2002: 50). Irigaray's long critique of the phallologocentrism of science and reason demands as much of a burden on the expresser of reason as on the claim to truth expressed, as it is a lack of self-reflection which is allowed to disappear in claims to reason and the speaking subject is delivered from accountability. Institutionalized reason – law, rights, truth – manifests human opinion, which maintains superiority via paths of external control. Manipulating Guattari's paths, these external control paths could well benefit from self reference. External paths of control seek to master not individuals but the abstract and unlived/unliving category of the human towards which all organisms must aspire to be granted affirmation of existence. They both evince the category of human as a myth or pure idea, while offering that myth as a transcendental absolute, conflating the superstitious with the logical. In these structures, there are claims about being but no actual beings, and the act of abstracting being from dividuated entities into a concept negates beings and life. If we navigate the lives of the world via Spinoza's understanding of will and Guattari's of desire, through the silent speech Irigaray advocates, we focus on dividuated instances of life as unique encounters where each life matters. The ethical value of an encounter can be measured to the extent that overarching pathways of mastery are avoided or dismissed in favour of mutual exchanges via heterogeneous modes of expression, where neither element subsumes the other nor, crucially, abstracts the other through converting its qualities to a knowability. So even if AR seeks 'reason' in its arguments for welfarist reform, the slaughter of the animal is evident as they can never win while remaining the object of knowledge.

Not utilizing animals is not negation: The age of the consumer anthropocene is also the age of the named activist. From terrorist (of which there are an infinite variety) to suffixing any and every form of practice with 'an' or 'ism', activism has been subsumed from performing acts to being those acts. Transforming the verb to the noun is itself an act of epistemological aggression, and this is seen in the maligning of abolitionists, where anti-vivisectionists are named terrorists and vegans are tree-hugging idealists who are traitors to the privilege of their species. The abolitionist movement as a form of activism is like any in that it is active due to its verbs and not the naming of its occupants, and like feminists, abolitionists are named thus as often to insult as to celebrate. The problem with being this noun which is unique to animal abolitionism, however, is that unlike feminism and other minoritarian studies, abolitionism advocates for literally trillions of others who the anthropocene adamantly refuses to hear. The activist becomes the enemy and there is no longer a differend victim. Abolitionists do not seek for nonhumans to be recognized, as stated above this subsumes them, but to hear them is, referring to Irigaray's claim, very explicitly possible. Because another's language is not our language, it does not mean it is not a language. But, most importantly, because we humans *can* do something which irrefutably harms another for no reason, it does not mean we should. This is a devastatingly simple statement. Almost all humans who advocate animal murder engage with a repudiation of this very simple statement. They focus on humans alone – themselves as humans and abolitionists as other kinds of humans (usually critically). AR theorists use human logic and human language to formulate human arguments for increasingly anthropomorphized victims of human actions, and meat, entertainment and other exploitative industries use human arguments to vindicate their actions. All of these, whether to liberate or oppress nonhuman animals, negate the animal. For an industry which operates death machines, the epistemology certainly resonates with this persistence of death. The nonhuman is not even given the gift of its own death, that death is abstracted for a 'reason' – we 'need' to eat flesh, drink calf food and so forth. Affirmation of nonhuman life can only come through what Irigaray calls the 'letting be' and what Serres calls a 'stepping aside', which is how he defines grace. Affirmation of the nonhuman other cannot occur in the human discursive games which rally and negate the physical being of that other. Affirmation is letting go of our use of the other. 'What is invoked in the phrase of freedom is not a power in the sense of an eventuality, but one in the sense of an ability to act, that is, an ability to be a first cause from the cosmological point of view' (Lyotard 1988: 121). Abolition activism is twofold in that it involves acts against our own species to cease the destruction of the nonhuman other, but in its ethical embrace of alterity, it involves lack of action towards the other (except, of course, the palliative care many rescue animals need) through letting be or stepping aside so the other may express. While the pragmatics will be local, individualized and tactical, the point is, by becoming abolitionists in our actions, we are affirming ethical newness between humans and the natural contract, negating the anthropocene so as to affirm the world. Veganism, antinatalism, artistic activism and other activities are easy, deny us nothing and create freedoms, so to see such practices as privation overvalues the repetition of patterns of mastery imposed by the industrialisation of the death of nonhuman others.

A note on tone

Like many manifesti, the tone of this manifesto oscillates between the colloquial, the academic and also the hopeful (perhaps even delusional) and the angry. The reader is invited to read with similarly inconsistent intensities. As this is a book which seeks to activate, the language was difficult to keep homogenous because theory and action often confront each other with a mingling of vulgarity and abstraction that is the nexus which constitutes the expression of wanting to continue the fight for the world in activisms of all kinds. While this manifesto shows a certain disdain for the species 'human', it also acknowledges that each human is a collective of multiple voices, multiple conflicting assemblages of disparate expressions, and that activist collectives are greater versions of these often dissonant emergences which nonetheless work towards creatively altering territories. This book has unashamedly embraced the assemblage expressions of my experience, my hope and anger, and philosophies, and is also in great part made up of the inspirations of the many other voices cited and mediated. I aspire to the reader accessing similarly multiple selves and so trust that the inconsistent tone will help tap into the volatile rhythms of activism rather than be read as a flaw. There is an inherent contradiction in a manifesto in that it demands absolutes because it seeks action that, in this case, mobilizes radical compassion through creativity, while also being deeply antagonistic to essentialist or generalizing claims. Yet, ultimately, the final claim is absolute and generalizing. This is the purpose of a manifesto, and so the contradiction asks for a suspension of the need for consistency due to the urgency of the condition of so many lives affected by human exceptionalism (including the demand for consistent human logic) while also attending to the creativity encouraged in service of liberating those lives.

1

Wither identity?

What does it mean to inhabit a post-world? We are in a state where we have been told variously we are already posthuman, have always been posthuman, should strive to become eternal transhuman, where subjectivity is long gone yet still subjectification and stratification, where one is made a subject and placed within a hierarchical strata, continue to make the lives of individuals, even recognized ones, precarious, vulnerable or absent. We are in a world where the struggle between minoritarian subjects has become as volatile as that between minoritarians (not minorities but those who have less access to power, overwhelmingly the great majority) and majoritarian systems. Feminists, as the largest and most diverse group of those who struggle not only with being bestowed an agency-driven subjectivity but also the desire for subjectivity at all, seem to be an obvious place to begin with the Charybdis that is the status of identity in contemporary political activism. Randomly and arbitrarily, our world has been generally bifurcated into two genders in spite of there being plenty of opportunities for divisions to occur elsewhere or as proliferations rather than as a binary. Race, sexuality, disability, class and continuing minoritarianisms augment all subjectivities as they are increasingly seen as being made up of minutiae of isomorphic choices of subjectificating binaries where there is a dominant term (usually white, usually male, usually straight and so forth) and the secondary term is 'everything else', which is coterminous with a perceived 'failure' to be dominant. Perception of failure has historically been marked as a failure to perceive at all, leading to various making-invisible of subjects that has produced in identity politics the various projects of representation of difference in order to be counted as human – legally, ethically and scientifically. This chapter proposes the ahuman advocacy of no longer wanting to count as human. This claim is contentious precisely because many humans and all nonhumans still await their time of counting. Identity politics has long been critical of posthuman philosophy's forsaking of identity for metamorphic becomings and transformative post-subjectivity, while posthuman philosophy's many critiques of identity (with which I stand) still struggles with how to acknowledge dark histories of oppression without perpetuating the identities to which they were victims. I will attempt to explore and pre-empt the later chapters' call to activism by addressing this seeming impasse, which I see as no impasse at all.

The main conflict between contemporary identity politics and post-structural politics is its own kind of beautiful contradiction. In the primarily USA-based groups which seek recognition, minorities and those disenfranchised demand a validation of underrepresented identities or an end to stereotypically and thus usually denigrative representations by those whose identity is not commensurable with that being represented. In what has been called the corporeal feminist school, the adaptation of post-structural philosophy has produced a more mobile form of identity, where becomings are preferred to atrophied subjectification. This latter school should in no way be considered unaccountable for the continued oppression of minoritarians (which is where its seeming contradiction occurs), but it seeks a polyvocal collectivity. I myself am utterly complicit in this oppression. What I seek here is a way to navigate my own aversion to identity politics, which many other philosophers share, while accepting that this aversion can insinuate a refusal to attend to those identity politics that, due to the conditions of many lives in various circumstances, are undeniably in need of address. The question of whether address means recognition is unclear. Linda Martin Alcoff and Satya P. Mohanty address the complexity at the heart of this seeming impasse: 'Obviously identities can be recognized in pernicious ways in classrooms or in society in general, for the purposes of discrimination. But it is a false dilemma to suppose that we should *either* accept pernicious uses of identity *or* pretend they do not exist' (2006: 7). Corporeal feminism generally sees identity as inherently utilized neither perniciously nor in a celebratory manner, nor even as non-existent or not useful. It does see a simultaneity that resists all either/or scenarios, and in this sense, configuring identities as becomings makes a palimpsest of both space and time. Spatially, we can experience, or even tactically configure, our existence as an immanent encounter with ourselves in connection with everything else as a series of relations which resist and refuse the subjectification we have been ascribed while being aware and attentive to the categories of ascription that we still occupy, because in this set of relations, the openness of others is questionable. We may be becoming but society still retains us in being. As Gilles Deleuze and Fèlix Guattari tell us: 'You will be organized, you will be an organism, you will articulate your body – otherwise you're just depraved. You will be signifier and signified – otherwise you're just a deviant. You will be a subject, nailed down as one, a subject of the enunciation recoiled into the subject of the statement – otherwise you're just a tramp' (1987: 159). Identity politics seeks not so much to change the signifying system – a project inherent to the ahuman manifesto – but to change the suffix signifiers and attempt to resignify the value and qualities of the signified, its organisation and collate the statement as one in order to produce collectives who can fight as one. As many before me have pointed out (from complex feminist critiques to white-knight male 'saviours'), this celebration of disorganisation is easy for two white privileged French men, but identity politics does remain within the syntax of Western white patriarchy, so can changing the signifieds be enough? Can we do both, in that spatially we are becoming while society's perception may be reminding us that we are depraved, deviant tramps, and so we simultaneously reclaim that by acknowledging the affects of such naming on ourselves and others? I would argue yes, because launching mobile subjectivity does not launch us into an entirely different world without history, and here is the temporal aspect of the contradiction. Our becomings have a long history, both collective and individual; we don't start from nowhere. So we can inhabit a line of flight without forgetting the trajectory from whence we came. Indeed, the very reason most minoritarians want to enter into becomings is because we do not wish the past to project a reiteration of our subjectivities and how they occupy the world in the future in the same way.

The criticism of fluidity, mobility and becomings in what is now called post-identity politics suggests what Paddy McQueen claims is an uncritical celebration of the essentially contingent and fluid nature of identity overlooks how these contingent norms are 'realized as deeply entrenched, bodily dispositions' that are 'lived and relived as inevitable, natural dispositions' (McQueen quoting McNay 2014: 82). Consequently, [Chantal] Mouffe's account of identity and her political vision of perpetual agonism fail to appreciate the ways in which entrenched social inequalities and oppression can result in deeply felt experiences of helplessness, disengagement and disempowerment. Simply highlighting the malleable, open-ended nature of identity does little to address this situation and fails to generate the kind of radical political agency necessary to remedy it. (2015: 78)

The proliferation of claims such as the above highlights three key issues with identity politics that may be uncomfortable for minoritarians to negotiate but which nonetheless retain minoritarians within the realm of the 'signified from without' even while we attempt to resignify values and qualities. The first is a certain (and I attempt to say this with tact and sensitivity which may ultimately be impossible) self-absorption whereby techniques of self – self-awareness, self-validation, self as part of a community of like selves – overwhelm any sense of the organism's connectivity to all relations within the world, both those with diminished capacity for expression (the less agential) and the oppressors. This reflects the very foundation of anthropocentric hubris, albeit majoritarians rarely show any self reflexivity, preferring to masquerade their self-interest as neutral universality.

The second difficulty with identity politics in this context is that attempts to make subjects visible and valid fails to account for the mobile state of capitalism and its signifying regimes which adapt and reshape the way society trains subjectivity to consume as representation, to self-realize based on patterns of purchase (of ideologies and objects) that put the subject in a state of perpetual loss and that actively fosters disengagement and disempowerment by making only power attractive and engagement only possible through aspiring to majoritarian manipulations of signification. This is why the 'add on' nature of minoritarian politics will continue, because capitalism will always find ways to oppress in ever more novel and ever more refined ways. The third issue with the pitting of fluid identity against identity politics is the most important for this manifesto and harks back to a divergence between posthumanism and the ahuman. In order for collective assemblages and relations to be ethical, we must cease privileging our own situation before and above all others, which can sometimes seem to be the very essence of identity politics – *my* identity. The ahuman *does* seek dehumanization because at its heart it seeks to dismantle human exceptionalism and make activism for the other – without necessarily seeking to know or apprehend or even be in proximity with the other – its primary technique in coalition with a general politics of differentiation rather than an endless taxonomy of difference. Here is why the work of Adams is so crucial. Her critique of those who argue 'humans first, then everything else' elucidates the perhaps understandable but inherently narcissistic nature of identity politics which joins it with all other forms of anthropocentric politics, including the most restrictive and eugenic kind. I am not suggesting that identity politics excludes as its major project. Many post-structural criticisms of any kind of subjectification, no matter how radical or transgressive, emphasize what is excluded when something is recognized if they hold on to issues of identity.

Foucault is deeply critical of this in his 'Preface to Transgression' (1998), because by speaking what is left out, the apex of the pyramid of signification remains the goal. The question becomes who will occupy the very limited space at the top because anthropocentrism stratifies just as it signifies, so even if there were such a phenomenon of a non-isomorphic binary or multiples, the struggle for supremacy would become the legitimizing drive rather than any openness to what is yet to be included, and all this before the acknowledgement that these categories are in constant flux, whether we want to accept it or not. Is making a minority manifest in a more accurate or truthful manner inclusive or exclusive? It will always be both and temporary. In this sense, perhaps we need an identity politics of discomfort rather than seeking the comfort of our identity becoming manifest. For an ethics of discomfort, Foucault states,

> A manifest truth disappearing not when it is replaced by another one that is fresher or sharper but when one begins to detect the very conditions that made it seem manifest: the familiarities that served as its support, the darknesses that brought about its clarity, and all those far away things that secretly sustained it and made it 'go without saying'. (1994: 447)

Minoritarians are the scaffold upon which power is built and which upholds what is seen as deservedly visible as the Vitruvian human, the white male (yes, who I am so frustratingly perpetually quoting I am aware). Ahumanism reclaims our darknesses; the dark continent of the realisation that we can see in the dark and are not your Eurydice so 'fuck you Sigmund Freud and we don't care to respond to your question of want Jacques Lacan'; Oswald de Andrade's magnificent

Cannibalist Manifesto of 'we will eat you colonialism'; the queerness of 'we will extinguish the species' heteronormativity; and the very darkest of the dark within which the most oppressed absolutely exist in the worst possible conditions so choke on your 'happy' meat and milk. Is illumination equality or resolution? Is a making visible of the most oppressed identities going to do enough, or is a making visible and transforming the conditions of living by connecting uncomfortably and without a template as to 'how' a more ethical technique? Becomings are the verbing of the world. They act and ask how; they do not define and ask what. I am utterly against the continued fetishization of minoritarian intensities which perpetuate so many post-structural becomings, especially those where the lived experience of the academic bears no resemblance beyond the page or the canvas or the screen to the lived experience of the other. And fighting for the other is an absolute luxury for many in a position of privilege, myself included. However, it is precisely when the dominant *and* the oppressed human other, in their infinite and specific manifestations (although the dominants manifestations seem somewhat consistent), aspire to the anthropocentric pinnacle of signification through wealth or power or even self-identification over all other practices of liberty *at the expense of the nonhuman other* that this manifesto says enough.

And enough is enough.

The nonhuman and human hypocrisy

'The animal rights movement has the misfortune of a modernist claim just as postmodernism displaces and absorbs modernist thinking … the autonomous, unitary human fades in the presence of postmodernism *except* at a meal' (Adams 2009: 61, 70). This powerful observable phenomenon strikes me reflectively as much as when I first read Adams's *The Sexual Politics of Meat* (1990), where she is astonished that a pet rescue shelter supporter serves ham sandwiches and a feminist conference serves all manner of meat, dairy and eggs. At this time, the word 'intersectional' had only just been coined, yet most feminists would be familiar with that particular mode of learning and experiencing feminism where race, sexuality, ability, class and other minoritarian considerations were inextricable from being a feminist. I need not rehearse the arguments that feminists have at their best always fought for the rights of other identities, identities which both intersect with female identity, such as women of colour, sexual minorities and trans rights, and identities which do not (e.g. the work done for AIDS victims by lesbians in the USA in the 1980s). Feminism has often found itself in situations where privilege is questioned, such as the struggle by women of colour to be heard among white and often racially blind feminism, and currently the tensions between so-called TERFS and trans women (much of which is valid, much of which is media-fuelled, and all of which seems to ignore the common oppressor of patriarchy) are often raised. These are complex issues for which I have not done justice and to which I shall return in passing, but they are all identity-based issues which remain within anthropocentric recognition discourse (which is, of course, also a discourse on safety, vulnerability, agency and rights but nonetheless via an anthropocentric social contract) because, ultimately, they all put humans first even when attending to human– nonhuman animal relations. There remains one absent referent which poignantly is exactly the name Adams in *Neither Man nor Beast* gives to the nonhuman when under the phallologocentric gaze. This absent referent is the nonhuman and our relations with them. Accessing philosophy primarily through feminism as a young academic, sitting down to a meal with respected feminists sometimes struck me like a family dinner where some member would suddenly launch on a racist rant or when you discover one of your friends is surprisingly a voracious homophobe. Harsh though this sounds, it is absolutely as Adams describes, a simple, observable exception that, while I am no logocentric, makes no sense to me in the simplest way. Except for one and only one likely hypocrisy of human exceptionalism that spans both identity politics and post-structural fluid identities (and here perhaps is where they do conform): as long as it does not affect me or my species (including its discourses), it does not matter. There are any variety of arguments and ophidian rhetorical configurations (otherwise known as excuses) which underpin the reasons why any and all minoritarians remain in the realm of what is known as the malzoan (those who mistreat animals by not being abolitionist vegans: *mal*=bad, *zoan*=animal life). The most common one is that which Adams cites as the 'humans first' argument, which holds true across philosophy and pychology, as humanist psychology thinks the 'humans first' approach is cognitively necessary for more empathy towards nonhuman animals, which clearly has no affect in ahuman thought. But Adams also cites the strangely amorphic malzoan 'I can't' argument, which is the arbitrary apology one gets at the table from nonvegans. Why do they apologize to another human whom they are not cannibalising? Here is the key that returns the issue to that above of anthropocentric-signifying systems. Here is why animal studies as a field is inherently unethical. With the exception of abolitionism, all discourse on nonhuman animals is between humans and ultimately reducible to being about humans – our wants, our 'needs' and our opinions and apologies. I have already written extensively on the ways in which Continental philosophy and posthumanism have failed the nonhuman animal (2012, 2014, 2017), but my targets were easier: posturing white male philosophers from whom I expected nothing. And this is a problem because feminism has long been expected, just as women themselves, to give more, do more, work harder and be better examples. So I would ask that this section be taken not as a symptom of that expectation, though it would be a lie for me to claim that I do not expect better from feminists of whatever gender, which is my problem, not feminism's. Perplexity at the cognitive dissonance remains. Identity politics has various 'human first' claims about race and gender and the impossibility of abolitionist veganism as culturally insensitive and economically unattainable, and posthuman theory claims that as identity is fluid one cannot commit to a single activist practice that is absolute. Neither argument seems more than a resistance to an accessible and immediate potential for ecosophical activism that could reduce suffering exponentially across the entire globe. The issue of culture is a human one and most often deployed by privileged white people about the impossibility of a phantasmatic pastoral indigenous society not being able to be vegan, hence somehow neither are they. It is anthropological semantics at best. The issue of race and feminism at the intersection as a socioeconomic issue is certainly valid, but the idea we need to repudiate animals to give racism and feminism justice is not. These intersections of oppression have been explored and abolitionist issues embraced by many theorists including Adams, A. Breeze Harper (also known as Sistah Vegan), Elena Wewer and Tara Sophia Bahna-Jones, and the argument between race versus abolitionism is a complex one beyond the discursive scope of the ahuman because it is human as the above theorists emphasize. The intricacies highlight the ways in which many arguments, discussions and seemingly endless discursive acrobatics all come back to humans amongst humans speaking about humans and what is best for them. Abolitionist vegans are consistently asked to account for themselves and rarely engaged for what they are practicing, which is an ethics of what Serres calls grace, which is leaving be:

> Whoever is nothing, whoever has nothing, passes and steps aside. From a bit of force, from any force, from anything, from any decision, from any determination … Grace is nothing, it is nothing but stepping aside. Not to touch the ground with one's force, not to leave any trace of one's weight, to leave no mark, to leave nothing, to yield, to step aside … to dance is only to make room, to think is only to step aside and make room, give up one's place. (1997: 47)

Leaving be is a tricky concept to which I will return (it does not mean ignoring, but it is careful in its navigations), but for now what is understood by leaving be is both actually activist *and* discursive. The entire animal studies oeuvre is founded on humans speaking, speaking for, speaking about, speaking 'with' animals. Posthumanism's turn to animals makes equivalences between our posthuman futures and perceived animal behaviours in a co-optive manner no better than becoming-woman. Abolitionist vegans' care for nonhuman animals is a care that liberates animals from the imposition of human expression that imposes and limits their affects to being interpreted only through human translation. We do not need to argue why nonhumans deserve this or that, be it based on degrees of equivalences with humans (no more dolphin and chimp fetishists who are not interested in the banal cow) or based on sentience (the 'dum(b)' animal argument). Nonhuman animals are here and they are here with no less right than us to the planet (although our destructive impulses which have altered ecological and environmental territories would make us more accountable). The modern and postmodern world no longer needs animals for human survival, although even if we did, what makes humans more special than animals? The old paradox of animal rights which despairs at 'they are good enough to act as equivalents in vivisection but not good enough to respect' is updated during the rise of veganism with the various new adages of malzoans known as 'omnivore bingo' – 'lions tho', 'cows will go extinct', 'what if you were on a desert island' (see vegansidekick.com for the entire exhausted list). These tedious arguments seem superficial and often amusing in their absurdity. They reflect a continuation of a number of disparate paths of philosophy and culture – the inexplicable and unlikely scenarios of moral philosophy, the phantasm of 'health' and techniques of the self where plant-based eating is mistaken for veganism and used to further control women's bodies (see Wright and Adams 2015), and the utilitarian argument that more humans want to murder and enslave nonhumans than do not. Ironic, considering a fully ecosophical utilitarian perceptive would have the hundreds of billions of nonhuman animals disagreeing with the seven billion humans who make up only 0.01 per cent of earth's life (Carrington 2018). The list could be extended ad infinitum and yet all of these discursive trajectories come from a common point, which is the centralization of human exceptionalism. Even issues such as 'welfare' and 'conservation' are for humans. The idea of leaving alone absolutely, the conclusion of human extinction, seems unthinkable because the idea of a world without humans is understood as an apocalyptic end rather than an opening of the world. Discourse is exhausting in the face of a phenomenally simple reality of grace, which is that right now, every moment of everyday, there is an opportunity for almost every human to not participate in the wholesale murder, torture and enslavement of nonhuman animals. The material actuality of what can be done relatively simply to alleviate and reduce suffering is astoundingly basic, yet the lengths to which anthropocentrics of all types will go to vindicate their malzoan practices never fails to surprise abolitionists. Because what we are fighting is a war, as Adams claims, on compassion, but increasingly between humans who identify as human and having human rights, and ahumans, which is how I would describe abolitionist vegans, who are fighting against their own species for organisms whose liberty would not necessarily benefit their own ahuman status but for whom they fight nonetheless. In some ways this can be understood, without wishing to set up new false dichotomies, between non-signified material reality (this animal you are eating was murdered – yes, in words, but the raw fact is on the plate) and the anthropocentric signifying practices which convert all experience into empty currencies and circulation of postmodern fads, values, beliefs and so forth. No individual's self-stylization, vegan or not, trend-follower or not, posthuman or not, can argue with the murder on the plate. There is simply no way to turn this into a symbol without denying the nonhuman their material living. Abolitionist vegans are not accusers. They may bear witness and make the malzoan account, but the act has occurred. The victim is on the plate, in the zoo, in the laboratory, starving in their decimated environment, hanging on the wall, worn on the human body. Lyotard states, 'By identifying oneself with the legislator who orders one's death, one nevertheless escapes the miserable fate of being the referent for every forthcoming phrase that may bear one's name' (1988: 100). Abolitionists have become the stand-ins for malzoan arguments for malzoan practices, where engaging in animal rights arguments or animal studies arguments vindicates the death in front of us, what Lyotard after the Athenians calls 'dying in order not to die'. The stakes are which human group wins the argument, not who will die or what will become of the future nonhuman animals destined to die (namely livestock, which currently make up 60 per cent of mammals on the planet, see Carrington 2018). The contentious spectre of creating equivalences between the current nonhuman holocaust and the Second World War holocaust is one vindicated by many, including lectures by Jewish Nobel Prize winners Isaac Bashevis Singer and J. M. Coetzee as well as in the work of Charles Patterson (2002). Marjorie Spiegel (1997) similarly launched the study of comparisons between slavery. I mention these not to digress but to show that even the most desperate attempts to show to fellow humans that we do not want or need this nonhuman holocaust, by those who experienced their own or empathize the most, show a rift within the discourse itself. This evinces that ahuman 'discourse' is already at play, coming as pleas as much as statements of fact, showing both the judicial self-interest which allows 'scientific' research to 'prove' we 'need' things such as dairy (funded unsurprisingly by the dairy industry, see Moodie 2016) and augmenting the social contract's obscuring of the natural contract which is without signification or subjection. Abolitionists, contrary to many perceptions, do not necessarily have a more intimate or empathic connection with nonhuman animals (though some may). Like women who have been told they are more emotional and therefore more likely to be maternal and caring, veganism has been met with charges of emotional discursive practice, affirming the logocentric practices of phallic, truth-claiming, masculine malzoanism. The roots of ecofeminism and the vital foundations it set are challenged today by postmodern playfulness with identity that aligns being an ally with being somehow feminized or less manly, which translates to less human. So the feminist man and the vegan man (whatever man means in this context) are aligned, and women are 'of course' more likely to be vegan due to their 'natural empathy'. The stereotypical and superficial anthropocentric designations which reduce everything to the standard isomorphic binaries with which we are familiar adapt for the postmodern posturing, where we now have people stating they are vegan with 'qualifiers' or men wearing 'I am a feminist' T-shirts while avoiding housework or fetishizing femininity. Adams's original critique that the postmodernization of modernist activist animal rights to animal rites as a spectacle of identity play is found everywhere in the enunciation of 'What are you, what am I?' Contemporary animal rights seem to have a lot to do with stating what one is rather than activism, although the rise of veganism and the availability of a variety of new kinds of food (which diminishes malzoan excuses) shows something that is more positive and more ethical than all the arguments humans have between themselves, which is the material reduction in individual consumption of the nonhuman dead and enslaved. (Unfortunately, this is offset by population growth, which will be addressed later.)

What does equality mean?

In many respects, equality has become a debunked myth both for feminists and for other minoritarians. It is usually aligned with identity politics and is not embraced by difference feminism or Continental philosophy. Equality is as much of a myth as the humanist transcendental subject, replaced with words like justice or access due to the presumption of verisimilitude in subjectivity which equality proposes – equal freedoms for equal persons. Difference feminism inspired mainly from the Continental school of thought tended to oppose equality with validation of difference and multiplicity. Both schools of feminism retained a deep commitment to the amorphic notion of equality as a politics of value and access, and in a somewhat old-fashioned turn, perhaps it is time to revisit what equality means on an ecosophical level. I am not following any established egalitarian systems or even a moral philosophy evaluation. I am using the term at its most raw and basic from an ecosophical perspective to ask a key question of contemporary ethics – when we say we desire equality, what could that really mean? Cynically, this is driven by my suspicion that even the best-intentioned human ethics are flawed due to their anthropocentrism. Frustratingly, it is driven by a sense that perhaps equality is not available, even theoretically, because it is simply an aspiration which is pragmatically unable to be enacted in activism.

Optimistically, the question interrogates sometimes shocking presumptions in anthropocentrism that can jolt us out of our complacency to become more creative in our adaptable activisms, because all we have are our imaginations when anthropocentric systems crumble. I use the word 'equality' over others inspired by Joan Dunayer's incredibly ahuman work on speciesism, and so it is to her that I will turn for the working definition of equality: 'All sentient beings (nonhuman and human) have equal value' (2004: 124). This simple statement includes two key components, one of which is problematic and the other transparently clear. The problematic term is sentience, as it is this term which has deep-rooted genealogy in anthropocentrism in creating the measure of equivalence between organisms, which is why Morten Tonnessen and Jonathan Beever prefer 'biosentience' where 'subjective experience is an undeniably ubiquitous characteristic of all living systems' (2015: 48). This is taken further in Christine Korsgaard's analytic philosophy work (2019) showing a new distribution of care towards equal value of the sentience of the other, whatever that may be, because it is a sentience we will never understand under its own conditions. Biosentience conforms more with the Spinozist argument that all living systems have unique capacities for expressivity and being affected, and exist unto and for themselves as singular manifestations of their own desire and will, consistently metamorphic both spatially and temporally. In this sense, all organisms and potentially organized environmental territories are biosentient. For Dunayer, 'Old' speciesist law, philosophy and welfare and 'New' speciesist law, philosophy and welfare both retain sentience as defaulting to equivalent to human sentience where the supremacy of the human goes unspoken. While old speciesism operates along the expected arguments around God and man being reflections of one another and the ensuing human exceptionalism arguments, even new speciesism measures by degrees of separation from the human, following the 'some are more equal than others' adage. The structure of hierarchy somewhat flattens but remains in a concrete form. Continued issues both linguistically and in terms of labour, slavery, rape and other oppressive actions against minoritarian humans are the only really equivalent systems of relevance. What happens to animals is also what has happened or is still happening to minoritarian humans. The template of hierarchy, whether flatter or more towering, is the retrospective structure that maintains all injustice towards humans and nonhumans, and this structure is the problem, not the nature of the entity considered for equality. Structuration of life itself is anthropocentric. It denies life in place of category, taxonomy, genus, species, gender, race, sexuality and ability. Individual expressions of organisms for anthropocentrism emerge through their preconceived category and are destined to be limited, even slaughtered, by the conditions and uses to which those categories ascribe them. This is the furthest from freedom. Life emerges without its own potential for expression when categorization subsumes it before its incarnation. Dunayer's most lucid transparent concept comes into play here – 'value'. All life is equal suggests that we measure a life and then argue how it 'lives up' to other lives, still supposing a life must be placed in a category before it is perceived. This field of equality maintains a demand for recognition before worth is evaluated. Dunayer shifts this focus in antispeciesist law and philosophy from welfare to abolition where value is equal. Value in contemporary global anthropocentric practices sees the nonhuman as expendable either because of its use for human consumption (from food to entertainment) or as collateral damage from development. The arguments of old and new speciesist laws become absurd when, as Dunayer points out, we realize they are always primarily about vindicating practices we wish to excuse but have no real reason for, particularly at this time in human history. Value is currently defined as value for humans. Inherent value as equal simply due to being remains uncomfortable or unthinkable for much philosophy, even those which espouse the emergent incarnation of life as beyond taxonomy (or, more apparent, this philosophy of life is pertinent, but the philosophers seem less inclined to practice activisms based off a non-speciesist understanding of the theory). Questions raised by animal advocates and speciesists within this structure are retrospective in their solutions, as Dunayer states: 'Until we reduce society's speciesism, we'll continue to treat the symptoms rather than curing the illness' (2004: 161). Equality in value makes no demands on the quality of the organism to be anything more than its own expression of what it is. Crucially, there is no centralized evaluating judiciary point of reference. So many ethical analyses hinge on the cessation of forcing the victim to advocate why they should not be the victim, which is concomitant with forcing any organism to also advocate why it should be allowed to be at all, to speak its value. The invisible centralized nameless, faceless god of humanist anthropocentric reason makes demands of all organisms without accounting for its own position and presuming its own neutral infinite wisdom. The value of the other cannot be considered equal when this anthropocentric god bases value on *value for the speaking majoritarian human*. Lyotard ask,: 'If the survivors do not speak, is it because they cannot speak, or because they avail themselves of the possibility of not speaking that is given them by the ability to speak? Do they keep quiet out of necessity, or freely as it is said? Or is the question poorly stated?' (1988: 10) The demand for the other to speak in order to evaluate its value is a form of violence, most poignant when the screaming of a nonhuman animal being murdered or the cries of a nonhuman animal being tortured are not recognized as language. The speech of the animal is not a testimony to evince worth, but ignoring it for convenience or seeing it as a Cartesian 'animals are machines' automated response is an undeniably vicious ignorance which directly emphasizes the unaffectability of the anthropocentric human by the expressions of other organisms that makes this scenario deeply unethical. To demand rather than express occupies the same unethical communication structure as to be unaffected by the expressions of others. Spinoza sums this up succinctly: 'I submit that the world would be much happier, if men were as fully able to keep silence as they are to speak' (1957: 30). Spinoza comments on the human body as an expression of the natural world as far more complex than anything which can be developed by human art, the mind or argument, claiming that the human mind is incapable of even contemplating the complexity of natural law (1957: 29–31). Both the exhaustibility of anthropocentric discursive systems and the hubris of not perceiving the most simple organism as beyond our capacity to know it absolutely are emphasized here. While science develops, the intrusion of anthropocentric interpretation will always prevent the value of the simple and the complex, concurrent in all life, from being appreciated as of equal value. The demands, the questions, are anthropocentric impulses. The silence, the letting be, can open us to non-speciesist occupation belonging to rather than owning of the world. Both old and new speciesist arguments would construct silence as evaluative observation and the demand to speech of the other – a speech that can be interpreted anthropocentrically – a requirement for equal value. Silence within the natural contract is silence and observation as cohabitation with care, symmetrical occupation. New speciesist arguments oppose the old in that they grant nonhuman animals negative rights (passivity, humans must speak for the nonhuman) rather than positive wrongs (animals are machines, animals lack agency, animals do not resemble humans). Zipporah Weisberg critiques the negative value activism of contemporary new speciesism as denying animals agency in their own futures, though the difficulty lies in how to listen and hear in ahuman ways to the less obvious pleas. She also critiques another trend in post-structural philosophies which afford all material, animate and inanimate, organic and nonorganic, certain 'agency' which is becoming a tedious inclination in certain areas of posthuman philosophy, where a chair is no different to a cow or a human. She claims,

> Remaining attached to the Kantian conception of agency only perpetuates anthropocentrism and is, in a sense, dishonest. Claiming that everything, animate and inanimate, is an agent or conflating individual acts with full-fledged agency purges the concept of agency of its political and ethical salience and threatens to obscure the urgency of the task at hand to protect animals from the atrocities we casually inflict on them as a matter of course. Asserting that agency is present in every conscious, sentient human and nonhuman animal, and that it manifests itself in a variety of

equally important ways, is imperative if we are to see the project of liberation through. (2015: 78)

Like Weisberg and Dunayer, I see the project as one not entirely extricable from human-focused liberation projects, primarily the shared denigration to use value for the dominant by which all minoritarians suffer. Like Weisberg, I see the liberation of nonhumans as a potentially anarchist or at least communist and decidedly anticapitalist project. However, unlike Dunayer and Spinoza, I am not convinced of the imperative for self-preservation to come before the equality of others. And here is where I may lose the reader. If all lives are of equal value, and some lives perpetrate more resource consumption or cause the liberty of other lives to be compromised, then is their value to be found in their absence rather than their preservation? Can annihilation be positive metamorphic change? The idea of the death of the human will be further explored in this manifesto, but within the context of this argument I make two claims. The first is that I am speciesist but only with reference to one species – humans. The second is that from an activist perspective, there is as much, if not more, ethical affectivity which opens the world to liberty of expression found in not valuing oneself as in valuing oneself. As I have already stated, this is neither martyrdom nor nihilistic despair. But if we are truly committed to an ethics of antispeciesist liberty, we have to face some unpleasant realities. Although individual unlikely scenarios are unhelpful even though moral philosophers continue to utilize them (would you die for a ladybird in x scenario and so forth), thinking ecosophically, it is almost impossible to vindicate the effects humans have on the planet as valuable in comparison with the detriment we have caused. So before I dig this particular grave too deeply to climb out of, I want to ask the reader to engage with the real-life requirements of thinking all organisms as being of equal value which involves ending the economy of the individual and the economy of self-preservation as primary to a world made up of diverse life.

Is life queer (or ... how queer is philosophy)?

I remain more committed to philosophy for activism than to identity. While identity, even in a relatively non-representational state, remains an almost necessary burden, it is due to the reverse of dialectics that this burden seems to pressure us most. What I mean is that minoritarians seek to become heard, to become visible, which is the right of all life, even if an individual life is choosing the right to remain invisible and silent as part of that liberation. The obligation to representation, inclusion and rights is a burden because it places burden on the oppressed. The enunciation of categorization, of subjectivity or species, does not come from the minoritarian though. It comes from power – the power to name, and the power of the name rather than the individual organism to signify value and potential, rights and space. The trick of phallologocentrism is to keep the other invisible and silent while binding the other in strictures of signification with which we must grapple in order to be seen and heard. Once again, like the nonhuman, we are struggling with an epistemic system which we did not create and within which we can claim no benefit. The ingenious double bind of ignoring the other while imposing qualities of subjectification is the paradox that produces identity politics and the proliferation of in-fighting that occurs between minoritarians in order to keep clashes between them rather than between those who impose and those who negotiate the impositions of representation – be it under, incorrect or grotesque. Of course, I have performed something of the same thus far in my critique of identity politics. Why do I expect more of minoritarans? Why do issues of gender and race, sexuality and disability, class and even species, find their interlocutors among each other rather than with the perpetual absent referent of the majoritarian God-man, the now almost mythical but altogether too real rich, white Western male? The answer is unclear. The direction of treachery may be important. Yes, I am a traitor to my species. But the shocking statistics showing white women voting right wing evince that repudiation of identity is not always the same between traitors. It can go in a number of directions. It does always involve treachery to identity, which for posthumanism has usually been considered a good thing. But perhaps not all posthuman identity treachery is good, when we see white women voting for violent misogynist racist white men, when we see gay white men espousing a return to traditional values and reverting to pseudo eugenics to explain away racism and poverty, when we see working-class people blaming refugees rather than the ruling class for their poverty. White feminism has acknowledged its racist complicity, even while struggling to overcome it, because it knows that commitment to dismantling oppressive institutions through good intentions alone does not work and cannot slough off institutionalized learned perceptions, but also because self-interest in the face of a misogynist world can seem enough of a hurdle to struggle over to make it through the day. Intersectionality welcomes all participants and fosters disagreement as a learning experience more than a failure of development. Personally, the minoritarian political system of which I have been most fond is queer theory. Admittedly, this is not the USA version of queer theory which has been adopted as a somewhat equivalent substitute to LGBTQI rights activism and of which many postmodern feminists are deeply suspicious because it erased lesbians as soon as it recognized them. My own work on queer has run with the very foundations of the word from both a temporal and spatial perspective. Queer has nothing to do with identity but everything to do with action. Queer *moves*. It moves over time, so identity is absent but a staunch commitment to minoritarianism remains. It moves in space because it is tactical and will advocate the most needful minoritarianism in any given space. Queer resists all subjectification and stratification. Self-interest can come from an accidental collision, but queer adamantly refuses to speak its own position of being, per se, over speaking a position of activism and advocacy which may or may not correlate with personal benefit. Queer is motiveless, which makes it dangerous to the majoritarian who masquerades their own motives behind 'logic' and 'neutral objectivity'. Queer in my use most importantly is never individual; it does not recognize a hierarchy or taxonomy of species. It is adamantly about the death of the human in order for the liberation of all life, defined in a non-discriminatory way. Chrysanthi Nigianni states that queerness is 'the force to affect and effect changes in the way one theorizes, its capacity to produce deviant lines along established thinking and disciplines, its ability to queer the queer, that is, to undermine the self, to resist any normalisation' (2009: 1). Colebrook evinces how queer theory as a *theoria* is incommensurable with identity politics (2009: 18–19). In Grosz's evaluation of why we need queer, 'difference, alterity, otherness are difficult concepts to incorporate into the humanist and phenomenological paradigm of oppression which seeks to recognize all subjects (or more commonly, *most* subjects) on the model of a bare general humanity' (1995: 211). Exit any potential for nonhumans to survive. For Noreen Giffney, raising the term queer means 'each question leads, not to a resolution, but to another series of questions, thus continually frustrating our will to know, opening up a space of and for desire' (2009: 1). For the very reason Giffney offers and due to the commonality of the word 'queer' being suffixed by 'theory', I argue that queer is a form of philosophical (anti-) identity that can be utilized for non-speciesist ahuman activism. For ahuman theory, the roles of the activist and the philosopher are the same: to activate change, to play host while dismantling the parasitic human, to create new questions that open the human to the natural world outside of the social contract. Serres states,

The philosopher is no longer right or rational, he protects neither essence nor truth. It is the function of the politician to be right and rational, it is the function of the scientist to be right and rational; there are plenty of functionaries of the truth as it is, without adding more, the philosopher does not wrap himself up in truth as in breastplate or shield, he does not sing nor does he pray to allay nocturnal fears, he wants to let the possible roam free. Hope is in these margins and freedoms. The philosopher keeps watch over unforeseeable and fragile conditions, his position is unstable, mobile, suspended, the philosopher seeks to leave ramifications and bifurcations open ... The function of the philosopher, the care and passion of the philosopher, is the negentropic ringing of the changes of the possible. (1997: 23)

Serres sees scientific classifications and the will to truth as a form of violence (1997: 97) and the role of the philosopher as one of care for the world beyond self. In much of his work, he critiques both politics and science for concealing their self-benefit behind the claim to truth, making truth, presented as an objective observation of phenomena independent of human intervention, a judicial enunciation deeply conservative of human benefit and value. The word 'truth' in this instance is the breastplate and the armour because it prevents accountability. In our post-truth world, the concept of truth as a contested site has become even more complex. Fake news and denial of truth is actual, while claims to truth are more often contingent and benefit various capitally driven arenas and values which retain traditional ideas regarding subjectivities, both human and nonhuman. The vulnerability of the philosopher is crucial, care of the fragility of the world is central to philosophical navigation and creativity, and this is no different to activism. The philosopher who espouses philosophy without activism is no philosopher. We must live our lives in our ever-changing philosophies. Enhancing or preserving our identities, no matter how minoritarian, may be useful and tactical, but if they are our goal then we are not philosophers. We are anthropocentric humanists and do not deserve to be activists or philosophers in a natural world. Non-reflective, non-reactive philosophy retains the issues from the past which catalyse its questions but seek to open new questions rather than resolve the old – the difference between difference and equality perhaps. The questions are queer. They answer with new questions. Serres suggests this is the drifting of philosophy: '*Ubi? Quo? Unde? Qua?*' (2015: 27) Where are we? Where are we going? Where do we come from? Through where are we passing? The perspectival attributes of these questions belie the queer nature of philosophy. 'Where' is temporal and spatial, it is in relation with our environment and its other occupants, it addresses the inflective qualities of always passing through and within when we meander. It is careful of the fragility of the world while being brave enough to keep asking and acknowledging the impossibility of answers in the face of activism being the actions of creating spaces for the expressivity of the other to flourish. Serres's invocation of passion reflects the politics of desire that manifests in queer theory. Passion like desire is a constant state. The clinamen is perturbed at different times in different ways that enhance our need to ask, 'Ubi? Quo? Unde? Qua?' Our philosophical passion, like queer desire, is beyond pleasure and unpleasure. The perpetual force of queer philosophy is always there, and it is always there in the politician and the scientist too, but at its worst, it manifests as the will to power, the will to anthropocentric exceptionalism.

Can ahumanism help us become a queer species? Does the ahuman represent an ephemeral interstitial species needed at this time to open liberty for a decimated natural world? Maybe I am trying to queer my species, but ultimately I am seeking to absent my species, both in reality and conceptually. So perhaps I am queering our relationship with our future. Disengaging from rigid systems of signification and subjectification enters us into a queer relation with the world because all we can do is ask questions. How do we listen to the world? How can we hear in languages and through expressions which affect us very differently to human significations? All the while we learn to hear while battling our own species in their determination to continue exceptionalism. Activists, abolitionists and those designated with less valuable identities have always been interstitial. The rich history of feminism, anti-racism, and all queerings based on alterity places us at the being-between location because Serres's questions have never been answerable for the minoritarian in the way traditional humanist philosophy can address them. The difference between the activist philosopher I offer via queer theory and Serres, and the traditional philosopher is not simply the shift from who and what to where but from philosophy as a kind of narcissistic luxury adventure in metaphysical searches for a vague abstraction tentatively known as 'truth' to philosophy as necessary to liberate certain real bodies from the truth of suffering, death and a life which can often be harder to live than no life at all. Queer philosophy has the responsibility of being philosophy for the other who has no need of philosophy, namely the nonhuman animal but historically coming from minoritarianism. It advocates without self-benefit. It activates without theoretical musings in the academe and at conferences limiting its reach. It is life as philosophy, a living organism that is philosophy, attentive, often mournful and despairing but driven by a commitment to the passion that is a passion for the world, not for the self. It is made up of anger, frustration and joy. It is adaptable and merciless to human exceptionalism, even in the face of being told it is absurd and deluded for wanting to end this species. It revels in the creativity required so no lament or sacrifice is privileged. It is time to demanifest anthropocentrism. It is time for humans to stop being human. All of them.

2

All action is art

In order to deliver ourselves from humanism and its posthuman tenets without fetishizing alterity, we have few trajectories that allow ascensions from subjectivity. Art as a creative force of affect is a way that can manifest in various guises not simply through what means are available but through the means unique to each entity, thus making art available to all depending on their specificity and assemblages. Can all action then, from an ahuman perspective, be understood as an imperative of art? This chapter explores ways in which art can be redefined to enhance the ethical nature of all action as expressive, affective, from personal actions to larger-scale activisms.

'But on both sides, on philosophy and science (like Art itself with its third side) include an *I do not know* that has become positive and creative, the condition of creation itself' (Deleuze and Guattari 1994: 128, original emphasis). Postmodern, hence posthuman, art (by which I mean a certain attitude to art, not the period in which art was made) revels in the 'I do not know' as an antagonism to criticism and a solicitation of unthought in the face of impression and catalysation without conversion to established signifying patterns. Postmodern attitudes to art have done the same, revisiting art from all histories and all artefacts not technically designated as art to see how their affects can dissipate the one who apprehends – but cannot comprehend – the art. Postmodernity has also performed the function of somewhat disengaging the art with artist; the death of the artist was simultaneous with the death of the author and remains so for those psychonaut seekers of becomings-otherwise through encounters with art that may be piqued by a name but are certainly not guaranteed by such. For this reason, the excessive, even accursed, effluvia of art in the age of capitalism, from Warhol's transformation from a studio to a reproductive brand and enhanced by the acceleration of art for money and as money, to the young British artists who make art as a comment only on money or on use value and goods, art is not always art in the age of the anthropocene. It is becoming more difficult to say what art is, but historically from Marx and Hegel, we receive an emphatically anthropocentric understanding of how it comes about and what its function should be. Tom Holert cites both:

> According to the Anthropocentric terms of Karl Marx's 1844 *Economic and Philosophical Manuscripts,* 'an animal forms only in accordance with the standard and the need of the species to which it belongs, whilst man knows how to produce in accordance with the standard of every species, and knows how to apply everywhere the inherent standard to the object. Man therefore also forms objects in accordance with the laws of beauty.' [Marx 2007: 276]. Put in original Hegelian terminology, 'art has to be linked to the deepest interests of mankind' [Hegel 1975: 7]. (Holert 2018: 62)

It is evident that post-structural philosophical understandings of the creation and function of art are at odds with those of modernist dialectics. Yet, while we remain in the age of the anthropocene and its capital techniques of measuring value and worth as both the purpose and outcome of creation and function, the status of art, especially art objects, continues to align itself more with the traditional anthropocene-confirming definition. This definition, here summarized by Marx and Hegel but commonly subscribed to, incidentally, accidentally and deliberately, expresses a confirmation of at least five trajectories directly attacked by posthuman philosophy and activism: the speciesist default that humans only are capable of autonomous creation; the phallocentric claim that humankind is mankind and thus human interests are primarily a certain kind of humans' interests; the universalization of anthropocentric perception as viable and true for the world; the connection between aesthetics (or beauty) and truth as an empirical and objective evaluation; the status of the (usually visual) object as a knowable vessel towards transcendental wisdom. And yet art still occupies a special privileged space of knowing/unknowing that separates it from science and philosophy. The art of words, of images, of sounds, in fact, what is known as 'the Arts', itself is becoming extinct in the age of the anthropocene due to the focus on STEM subjects being useful within the academe and industry. Simultaneously, this precarious and destructive set of self-automating systems of university, industry and government which rely on the new gods of STEM are what invigorates contemporary (always contemporary) activisms.

Activism is currently the most urgently needed action in the world for two reasons, which are also its two problematic qualities. The first is that the accelerated globalized forces of the anthropocentric world are preceded by the destruction they are not even aware they bring seemingly until it is too late. This is due to a number of factors not limited to postmodernity's distortion of time which continues to masquerade as causal chronocentrism, the jubilance in futurity that facilitates techniques of immortality found in everything from human reproduction to industry scaling-up and post-death upload/cryosciences, and a sort of artistically admirable tendency to experiment and 'see what happens' but due to anthropocentric hubris, with no thought to accountability or affectivity of experiments. Second, structurally activism repudiates structure itself. Because the world is increasingly both temporally fast and spatially simultaneous, large-scale political or even revolutionary movements are dubious in the ways they reflect the very structures they seek to dismantle, and impossible due to their development and implementation becoming defunct before it has been activated. Activism now is local with far-reaching effects, viral rather than ubiquitously recognizable, actively creative rather than reactive because logics of dialectics are no longer seen as effective or relevant. Activism is strangely specific, unique, tactical and polyvocal. It makes the concept of thinking a collective difficult, especially one which seeks to dismantle the anthropocene. For as long as there has been feminism, its tactics and applications have been locally adaptable and polyvocal; for as long as there has been anti-racism, activism has had to manipulate its particular actions based on location, time and issue, so these features have always been present within activism. Logocentrism has deemed this rhizomatic plane with quickened nodes, pressurized intensity points and fluid tides as faulty because traditionally new political options come as singular imposable structures for change. This demand not only homogenizes the globe and all its people but also is inherently ignorant of the network relational nature of ethics which is premised on dividuated encounters between more-than-one, their affects and the opportunities for liberty and freedom they facilitate across the world as a series of infinite assemblages, each of which, while connected in their entirety, have specific needs and constitutions. The ahuman encourages further, deeper ecological activisms come to the fore, which is why it can seem to privilege abolition and environmental network activisms over identity politics (and in many ways it adamantly does). Any kind of earth activism, and especially the rise in earth activism in post-anthropocene political revolution-seeking, attempts to put into dispute the two-player game of which Serres speaks. Inherent in Serres's critique that all contracts are social contracts, he emphasizes that the anthropocene creates the appearance of options and of conflict by opposing two players. Of course, the parallels for activism are clear – the minoritarian against the corporation. This continues the anthropocentric tendency to act as if 'the concrete world behaves as if we made it; similarly the money we mint and the projects we undertake act toward us as if we have not produced them' (2014: 29). The first example of the two-player dialect of combat is a familiar one, our world in which the little person, the oppressed, the individual, is in combat with the abstract machine of the institution. This fallacy of perception behaves as if these institutions are not man-made creations, no different from artistic creations, simply deployed for another purpose. It also behaves as if the world is 'for' the individual, exploiting the narcissism which the activist risks if all politics is focused on the personal identification of the activist. The activist in this scenario is a result of larger signifying structures of signification (designation from binary indices) and subjectification (designation on the social hierarchy) so their identity was never theirs anyway, and demanding its access and recognition is less an act of creative artistry than a risk of obedience towards subsumation into the abstraction of signification that is no less abstract than money. For Serres, there is a third player, and this player is the most important for ahuman activism both as an artistic and ethical impetus. He calls it Biogea:

> The game with two players that fascinates the masses and opposes only humans, the Master against the Slave, the left versus the right, Republicans against Democrats, this ideology against that one, the greens versus the blues …, this game begins to disappear when a Third party intervenes. And what a Third party! The world itself. Here quicksand, tomorrow the climate. This is what I call 'Biogea', an archaic and new country, inert and alive, water, air, fire, the earth, the flora and fauna and all the living species … International institutions in vain perpetuated those two player games which remain blind or harmful to the world. Who will have the audacity to found an institution where Biogea will finally be represented and have the right to speak? (2014: 30–31, 32)

Biogea is the canvas, the material, the muse, the impossibility of representation, the ethical other, the matter of self, of activism. It is the materiality which expresses the world but from the natural order, in absolute repudiation and disinterest of the human expression of the world as signified nature. Biogea has qualities which solicit ahuman becomings that collapse art and activism into necessary symbiosis. Ahuman activisms which enhance the natural and forsake human exceptionalism are dealing with a twofold radicalization of the need for representation and recognition. Traditionally, both political movements and art negotiate representation very differently. Political activisms based on identity politics demand recognition in a world that refuses to see them and often uses art in order to both self-represent and elucidate the blind spot they occupy in dominant culture, asking that culture to reflect on its own self-blinding therebycreating a double affectivity of introducing the unseen into the world of subjects and making that world aware of its own power impositions and denials of the other. Postmodern and posthuman art often seeks to dismantle the power in and of recognition through representation, seeing representation and recognition, even of self, as variously a myth of humanist transcendentalism, of ownership of the other, of knowledge as a wrangling form of potestas. Against dialectic art objects, postmodern art is what Lyotard calls 'the revolt of represented things' (1998: 90), where 'representation is thus assumed to be an energetic set-up, whose ruin would be that of the subject and of power. The problem of theatre and of "figurative" painting is no longer set out as a problem of knowledge or learning, or even of truth, but as a problem of power and force' (1998: 91). Activist art inspired by self-authorisation frequently engages both representation and misrepresentation in the service of power or force, to combat the forces which oppress and conceal the other. Inclusion matters, but no correct representation or apprehension is assumed as this risks essentialization, so most activist art continues to embrace polyvocality of expression even when belonging to the same loose identity activism. Activist art shares with postmodern art a refusal to representation, an engagement with power as much as aesthetics, but diverges in seeking the appearance of what has not appeared. This insinuates the risky task of inclusion. Being included in the register of the anthropocene is to be perceived anthropocentrically. Incremental requirements for a certain kind of aesthetic logic, belonging to the long-critiqued (mainly by feminists) world of oculophallologocentrism, are involved in being included. This means inclusion is always through anthropocentrically established dominant terms and so is absolutely without any ethical address towards the other, and is thus no ethics at all. Activism is more than just wanting to join the club of the dominant, yet the social contract seems to think this is both what is coveted and what is enough. The two-player game remains.

Beyond this, what happens when we are fighting for an other for whom we cannot, must not speak, the other we can never access? If posthuman art at its most basic level is something that has no claim to universalizing anthropocentric truth, then ahuman art takes that fiction in order to formulate activisms for the entirely unknowable without seeking to represent and nomenclature them, without validating the natural through inclusion or assimilation, comparison or objectification. Ahuman art may need to defy basic tenets of art and activism – art without being an object, activism without a goal or endgame. In their introduction to *Art in the Anthropocene*, Heather Davis and Etienne Turpin are adamant:

Nevertheless, using the Anthropocene to simply restate one's political commitments more emphatically, without addressing the pressing questions of population growth, technological interdependencies, and the contingent obligations of human settlement patterns, is an exercise in ideological futility; finding new approaches to posing problems is the work of both making art and making theory in the Anthropocene. (2015: 7)

Ahuman theory disanchors itself from philosophy's will to knowledge as power; it makes the demand that all theory becomes artistic practice in its expression as a form of fabulation, a new mode of unthinking, tactically and ephemerally remaking the world to cause beneficial territorial shifts. In this sense, Davis and Turpin are right to almost collate art and theory, as differing manifestations of a singular mode of expression, as activism which makes no universal claims and imposes no organisational structures from which both the activism and the original subjects and objects emerge. Art and activism share this unmaking of the world. Unlike the negativity found in the calamitous disclamations around the anthropocene within its particular definitions or the focus of its detrimental effect (capitalism, ethnocentrism, biotechnology, environmental degradation), art and activism see the perceived dreadful impossibility of the task beyond deconstruction and lamentation. This world falling to pieces, this world on the brink of destruction, offers the ripest opportunities to unmake what we already know of it because to know it as it is and thus either to try and perpetuate that earth or fix it to return it to some perceived glory is as fictitious as welcoming the world as being unmade by humans, materially and actually, and so let's unmake it *differently* by exploiting the gaps and hollows created, the losses of meaning, the end of transcendental guarantee that art will elucidate some absolute truth by which we will be delivered from living in obscurity and darkness. Our anthropocentric world is dark and we must learn to see in the dark and create new modes of perception, just as activism demands that we set upon courses of action towards change without being entirely sure what the results will produce.

Art and activism now place us in a very strangely non-secular state. In an almost inverse action to that I address in Chapter 4 as occulture, which leads to activism through new commitments to traditionally non-secular mythologies but without dogma or actual faith, ahuman activisms are almost or somewhat religious acts of art in three of their shared intensities. The first is hope. It is entirely easy, even logical, to despair in this epoch. Contemporary psychology is currently demarcating the post-traumatic stress disorder found, for example, in many new animal rights abolitionists (Levison 2016; Lizik 2015), which frequently leads to depression and suicide, and certainly haunts most of the thoughts of abolitionists surrounded by reminders of the constant suffering and death nonhumans are prey to perpetuated by our own species. Despair is to be expected and is co-present with hope rather than opposed to it. Despair which catalyses the 'there is nothing to do' is also what ignites 'we must do something' which is founded on hope. Hope in activism is amorphous, and especially due to its anti-capitalist, anti-(mono)causal aspect, it may have short-term goals which are aspired towards and long-term paradigm shifts but at the moment these seem impossible, activism changes its art to adapt and reorient in order to reinvigorate hope rather than give up because the same paths taken lead only to despair or atrophy. Hope is deeply reliant on art in that it demands imagination and metamorphosis to keep mobile rather than the mimetic resemblance of all activism to follow the structure of other 'isms' and political causes that can risk repeating the same outcomes (or lack thereof) and frustrations. Jacques Rancière states of art: 'So the principle of the anti-mimetic aesthetic revolution is not some "each to his own", confining each art to its particular medium. On the contrary it is a principle of "each to everyone else's"' (2007: 104). Activism can only be artistic if it is not used to restate or reinstate political commitments and identity politics mimetic towards established rubric. But to develop activist actions based on nothing that has gone before, the activism that taps into the chaotic potentiality of the necessary rather than the designed, relies on hope because it has no narrative upon which to reflect and thus no possibility of evaluation against which it can be measured. It does, however, live in hope without these logocentric patterns and does not consider itself as destined to fail because of the repudiation of mimesis. Just as art theory increasingly values the aesthetic rather than mimetic (not necessarily in practice but in perception and relation with the spectator), becoming what Rancière calls 'inhuman' in that it no longer concerns mimesis of humanist ideals, so activism uses this artistic aspect of aesthetic creativity to blaze new lines of flight towards changing territories and tactics because mimesis shows us that anthropocentric activism leads to the reiteration of anthropocentric goals – more reliable, perhaps, more pay-offs guaranteed – but this form of activism by its nature cannot concern the unknowable other. Like delusions and dreams, which are entirely at home in art (both liberating and propaganda) but not acceptable in the so-called real world, the unmaking and remaking of the world through minor revolutions happens with hope.

The second non-secular intensification is the impetus to the delusion that is hope. This is faith. If hope is the action of activism without a rulebook, then faith is the commitment to action being better than apathy or atrophy. Like hope, which is never explicitly a set hope 'for' something, faith is not a faith 'in' something but rather a faith that there can be a world that does not behave this way forever – more precisely, the humans of the anthropocene will not always be so anthropocentric. Ahuman activism is faith in ahumanism which is, of course, a faith in nothing except there is more than the anthropocene and anthropocentrism. It is everything outside of anthropocentrism that humans can do, but nothing is set in stone, so from a representative point of view, it is faith in nothing, and from an aesthetic artistic point of view, it is faith in everything that could be thought. The impossibility of art, be it the blank page before the philosopher and writer, or the blank stage of the playwright, or the blank canvas or slab of stone or raw materials of the artists, is the location of faith that the materials available can be transformed into a new mode of assembling the world. This is also true of activism. No special tools are needed, just a reassembling of what we already have to operate new waves of change. Rancière emphasizes,

> There is no appropriate language for witnessing. Where testimony has to express the experience of the inhuman, it naturally finds an already constituted language of becoming-inhuman, of an identity between human sentiments and non-human movements. It is the very language whereby *aesthetic* fiction is opposed to *representative* fiction. And one might at a pinch might say that the unrepresentable is lodged precisely here, in the impossibility of an experience being told in its own appropriate language. But this principled identity and the inappropriate is the very stamp of the aesthetic regime in art. (2007: 126, original emphasis)

This quote leads to the third non-secular element of activism as art, which is belief. But this is adamantly belief unto itself and *not* belief in a preceding system or thing. Rancière points to the inappropriate and impossible, both of which belong to the episteme of art where the unthinkable can come into being, the fictive becomes flesh and the appropriateness of art is in its capacities to discomfort and discombobulate without affirming or enlightening traditional ideas. Activism can never represent its goals because to do so would involve speaking for the other as if goals are shared and understanding of experience resonant, symptomatic of the narcissism in many visibility projects in identity politics but if they were to be made visible by an assimilating majoritarian. This is especially so in reference to activisms which concern others who cannot speak for whatever reason, where activism often involves ceasing the behaviours of dominant humans rather than empathizing with or understanding the suffering of the victims. Examples range across every kind of voice which the anthropocene refuses to hear, including nonhuman animals, trafficked women and children, civilian victims of war, developing-world workers, environmental systems, and in the West victims of domestic space violence both human and nonhuman. Representing the suffering of these entities may make humans feel something, but if it is representative, it makes the witness feel only in relation with their own situation. Responses range across Lyotard's four silences with which the differend is met in times of unbearable and unrepresentable anguish: I wasn't there; it didn't happen; I cannot speak for the other; there's nothing I can do (1988). Belief repudiates all four of these without exchanging them for their opposites. It also believes there is a position from which we can never perceive but which demands our assistance nonetheless and we should and can open spaces for liberty of the other without assimilation or converting that other to an equivalent to the majoritarian human. It is the doing of grace, the acknowledging the being of the other in the letting be, the creating space for in the stepping aside. All established language is anthropocentric except perhaps the language of art which is, for Lyotard and Rancière, the language of the unrepresentable and unspeakable to which we nonetheless must bear witness. This language is a loud call to activism, albeit in an ahuman language. And thus our actions must take similarly ahuman forms, which require a belief that doing something is better than not doing so, even while hazarding the risks of encountering the other and slipping into the anthropocentric mode so the other is once again closed off. Art and activism introduce a something that wasn't there in that form before. Both are manipulations in this world, *of* this world, to create what is unthinkable, in the hope that it will change the world, with the faith that the world will change and keep changing (which it always already does, but, problematically, the patterns are repetitive) and in the belief that this is better than either doing nothing or aligning politics with traditional, established patterns because they are seemingly more logical.

Activism invokes styles of fiction and fabulation. Practical activism without utopia still needs that which is not yet real, the made up, the dreamed of. Additionally, activism involves occupation of an imagined other, without bearing claims to know the other or their needs. The other becomes an imaginary friend, a character whose function is operational but whose affects may never even be encountered, especially in activism which involves peoples from other geopolitical locations, nonhuman animals and ecological environments. Activism demands imagination of others without quickening them into a knowable form. It requires the thinking of relations which do not exist except in the mind of the activist and their subsequent expressions of political force. Activism often benefits from corporeal and physical operations far removed from the theatre of traditional political debate or even protest. It taps into strange manoeuvres, more akin to dance and mime than rhetoric and semiotic seduction. Activism is clandestine and illegible, because change in relations and liberties takes precedence over the structure of the strategies and their goals. Activism is not informatic. It does not transmit bits of information. Rather, it creates new expressive territories of infidelity to dominant operational regimes. Guattari states,

> If I make a gesture it must relate to a text that says 'Is it appropriate to make this gesture at this point?' If my gesture is incoherent there will be, as in a computer, some written or digitalized device that will say: 'This person may be mad or drugged, perhaps we should call the police, or maybe he is a poet: that person belongs to a certain society and should be referred to a written text' ... the whole evolution of systems of enunciation tends toward the individuation of enunciation and toward the degeneration of collective arrangements of enunciation. In other words, one moves toward a situation where the entirety of complex systems of expression – as in dance, tattoo, mime etc. – is abandoned. (1996: 15–16)

Activism which involves the centring of the making visible of the self as defined by signifying systems falls into a twofold bind. The first is that the enunciative function is created as a single mode of 'exchange' (never entirely reciprocal) by which the dominant agrees to listen. But the enunciating activist must now be committed to their one kind of subjectivity and one issue based on their speaking as a singular for the many for whom their image is assumed to be an icon of the needs of the multiple. The second is that in this false dialectic, the dominant enunciator remains abstracted. The enunciator who decides if someone is an artist or another kind of epistemologically incarcerated subject, such as a drug addict or insane or a terrorist in the case of the way the world's governments and media designate animal abolitionist activists, feminists and freedom fighters, is a single social representative of a set of rules developed by humans but for which no single human will take responsibility, nor will they account for or change the rules. This reflects Hannah Arendt's critique of the Law of the Church and its effect on government, whose power 'solved the problem, in other words, within the given frame of reference in which the legitimacy of rule in general, and the authority of secular law and power in particular, had always been justified by relating them to an absolute source which was not of this world' (1964: 160). Capitalism and the abstracting mechanisation of semiotics circulate edicts and enunciations in the service of resonances of power so that heterogeneous levels of enunciation become homogenous motives for an anthropocentric world in self-service. This makes their motivations jar with artistic asemiotic functions which operate in the service of quality of affects, hoped for and unknown. This has been known from Louis Althusser, Foucault and Guattari, and their long critiques of the various apparent divergent agencies of control who have a single expression of power and a single perceptive mode. But these biopolitical control mechanisms have to recognize the form of disruption at least minimally in order to insert them into a heterotopia, be it actual or epistemological. The madness of the artist is a privileged one, because it remains licit within most circles of the apparent free West (itself a utopic claim but one which is necessary to attend to the increasing strangulation of the artist in many other areas of the world). Yet the artistry of nature, the way in which nature orders its elegant chaos, the polyvocal and imperceptible complexity of biogea, is sacrificed with ease by the anthropocene, not because it is illicit but because it is inconvenient. Anthropocentric expansion and encroachment, known politely as development, massacres nature because nature is not perceived as an independent and valid mode of expression(s) but as chaotic wilderness. Ecosophy listens intently without translation to these modes of expression and makes space through its activist tactics for these expressions to explore. For this reason, the art of activism involves both the passivity of such tactics as boycott and activist volition such as direct action.

Ecosophical activism adds the advantage of fighting for the unknowable other, thereby swerving away from the reification of new kinds of oppressed subjects and how they are made docile by the state's many signifying systems, from biopolitical to simply being disappeared, to resisting any form of single enunciation. The earth demands different asemiotic modes of expression, otherwise we remain in the social contract talking about nature as if it is external to us. It returns to the human-to-human speaking about the other, where the other is simply an object of knowledge, use or exchange. Complex ecosophical systems, like complex ecosophy, perceives the anthropocentric system as one within an infinite biogeic mesh. We cannot perceive these other languages and modes of expression, but we do live in relation with them and we are imposing a terrifying effect upon them. Deleuze and Guattari's often misunderstood as

fetish or metaphor 'becoming-animal' shows the difference between
the human and the human's cohabiters on earth: 'the metamorphosis
is a sort of conjunction of two deterritorializations, that which the
human imposes on the animal by forcing it to flee or to serve the
human, but also that which the animal proposes to the human
by indicating ways out or means of escape that the human would
never have thought of by himself (schizo-escape)' (1986: 35). In this
brief statement, Deleuze and Guattari describe the second of three
elements of animal metamorphosis stories which assist in attaining
minor literary styles, that is 'to stake out a path of escape … to find a
world of pure intensities where all forms come undone, as do all the
significations, signifiers, and signifieds, to the benefit of an unformed
matter of deterritorialized flux, of nonsignifying signs' (1986: 13).
Literature as an art form must attain this undoing in order to enter
a becoming-animal. The way both Kafka and Deleuze and Guattari
use animal is not the fetish object or even the fetishized system now
co-opted by much posthuman art and philosophy. They stay with
the very vague word 'animal' because they mean nothing more than
no-longer-human. Becomings don't know their becoming (and, of
course, becomings never become proper). The animal, which animal,
what animal, what is an animal? The ethical aspect is adamantly
highlighted in the earlier statement – an animal is something that
flees from the human because it knows it will be used or abused. It
has no other definition. The human imposes. The animal proposes.
Bearing witness to the fleeing animal (and allowing the animal to
flee) can help us in becoming-animal because it helps us to perceive
our power and imposition while showing the wonder of that which
refuses to be perceived for whatever reason an accidental encounter

with an animal may elucidate in that organism's fleeing. The same could be said, and in Deleuze and Guattari's volumes of Capitalism and Schizophrenia is said, of any minoritarian not privileged by anthropocentrism – women, children and so forth. Fleeing as an automatic response seems somewhat depressing, but we cannot blame the earth and its occupants from shrinking from our ever more encroaching imposing systems. We should definitely be asking why nonhumans and the world shrink from us. The techniques we use to facilitate fleeing as freeing are acts of activism and grace, and in order for them to be also acts of artistic becomings they must involve the undoing of anthropocentric tactics of inclusion because any inclusion of any organism, human or not, into the human taxonomy of so-called human rights or even the rights of life and the earth is destined to fail because it will always remain victim of human territories, including the bodies of the other and the earth which the human territorializes with anthropocentric knowledge even while claiming that we are giving nonhumans and minoritarians the rights they deserve, which correctly translates into the rights we have decided they can have because they don't inconvenience us too much. Becoming-animal in this instance is a call to activism that undoes what we know about how we fight. It involves fighting in new ways for things both material and ephemeral – material in their existence and in the urgent and real devastation to which they fall victim at human hands, and ephemeral because their existence belongs entirely to them and does not need to prove its value or even its evidence for us to develop tactics for their liberty. Activism via art repudiates the solipsism of the social contract between humans about the world, where all epistemes become judiciary independent of their unique claims to reality or truth. It dares to encounter without a need for illumination or transcendence the alterity of urgent causes which plea for urgent action in a language imperceptible by the dominant (or deliberately ignored depending how cynical one is feeling about being human or becoming-ahuman). An earth democracy involves unthinkable combinations within nature, of agreement and joy without resonance that operates within mirroring signifying regimes. Joy in incommensurability is the call to the need for activism, being confounded as to how to express that joy through activism is the artistic aspect of the action. Rancière states, 'The *demos* is ever drawing away from itself, dispersing itself in the multiplicity of ecstatic and sporadic pleasures. The art of politics must regulate the intermittency of the *demos* by imposing intervals which place its strength, at a distance from its turbulence, at a distance from itself' (1995: 15). In order to enter into a becoming-ahuman, to rise up against the anthropocene and its malignant destructive expressions of political violence and apathetic semiocapitalism which deny the materiality of the organisms who suffer and turn our politics into narcissistic seeming necessities of self-preservation, we have to think outside of human systems. This is the basic tenet of art, and art offers as many unheard undoings as nature, where we can meet nature to dually attack the exceptionalism of the anthropocene.

Art is life

I am neither so dumb nor so animistic to think that Nature is a person. (Serres 2006)

What is art *for*? In his revisit of *The Natural Contract*, Serres shows the ways in which anthropocentric social objects are utilized for anthropocentric values, and the objects become iconic of those values – satellite for speed, atomic bomb for energy, internet for space, nuclear energy for time (2006). Serres demarcates these modern objects of thanatocracy as detritus, objects laid to waste in front of us as a result of the thanatos that drives modern technology and capitalism to ascribe the dimensions of the earth as anthropocentric dimensions of production and value for industry, law, profit, knowledge. Anthropocentrism attends its worship of the new social dimensions of space, time, energy and speed via the objects that not only represent their reattribution from nature but also form a strange relationship with their essential 'waste status' – anthropocentrism creates things, and as they deteriorate and lay waste to the earth, humans move on, ignoring the affects of past technogods to seek new objects. The energies and the leftovers of the anthropocene continue to destroy the world in their decaying tendencies or perpetuated drives while we pretend these obsolete icons of human superiority no longer cause affects. These so-called useful items – useful until they are replaced, in spite of their continued degradation and dissolution into the world, their polluting leftover status – as objects of worship share in common the utility of a pornographic form of idol worship. They are absolutely necessary and the new object promising futurity and the perpetuation of humans even as they appear. The moment they become obsolete, they are not only discarded but also despised, and our climax leaves us with a dirty guilt as to have been so foolish to think they would satisfy us, but surely the *next* object will. For anthropocentric semiocapitalism objects for consumption, technofetishism or abstract informatic knowledge are perceived as art because they hijack our ways of believing. They do not differ between themselves; there is no unique quality between the objects of thanatocracy, only the continuation of the anthropocentric impulses they perpetuate. That is what these objects are for – the anthropocentric impulse. And so what is art for? Art is, of course, inherently useless. No one who believes in art believes that the financial value of a piece has any relevance so we need not engage that idiocy. Nor does the artist have much use beyond another object become an icon for worship. The artist is currency. Yet we are told in the current higher education climate the art degree is useless, the humanities are useless. STEM subjects are useful. Useful *subjects* in both senses of the word. The artist as subject is potentially useful because you may become famous. The art is left behind. The art piece only transforms into the art object when some price is ascribable to it. Subjects and objects redefining the dimensions of the earth. But the artwork, however it manifests, from a painting to a collective protest, is there ephemerally and without subject or object, to give. Without will, without intent, art gives.

> The use of the terms 'data' and 'given' in philosophy thus reveal that the objective or external world gives for free and asks nothing in return. Consequently, the knowledge link becomes parasitical. The subject takes everything and gives nothing while the object gives everything and receives nothing. Knowledge is then treated as disinterested in turn. The active or technical relation to the world exploits it and that is all. We did not know we were acting as parasites or predators. What appears normal, usual, commonplace in knowledge or action becomes scandal and abuse as an exchange. (Serres 2006)

Anthropocentrism takes and does not account for what it leaves behind. The corrosive effects of the left behind cannot be considered art, the means by which those effects could be curbed and the earth cared for definitely are artistic. For Serres and for the ahuman, the only object is the earth. Ahuman art must be for the earth, for every relation. It must account for the material affects it produces that occur on a cellular level, so sustainability and use of labour, nonhumans and other potentially non-consenting aspects is a necessary consideration (see Lockwood 2018 for the rise of vegan fine arts). It follows the tradition of activism as giving to rather than taking. Hence, why identity politics is detrimental to activism – taking control for oneself within the context of what is already available ignores the only object, which is the earth and which is every relation within it, and continues the subject–object dialectic that sees all struggles as struggles between a dominant and an oppressed on a micro and macro level. Certainly, ahuman activism takes because it takes from the anthropocene all power. Only those who wish to maintain anthropocentric power could perceive this as a taking. Activist art and artistic activism create chaosmotic ripples and flows that unravel anthropocentrism and open us to the 'object'/superject earth. This would not be a privation unless the parasite does not want to reciprocate. Art involves thinking tactics and techniques that undo any ability to impose an object–subject relation onto a situation of alteration of dominant anthropocentric paradigms. If successful in this navigation of relations, activism prevents the anthropocentric backlash of redeposing an us–them dialectic and creating new false antagonisms. Artistic activism/ activist art is free. It is also worth nothing and so is beyond any market. The changes in potential escape routes, opportunities to give and capacities to transform mean there is no recognizable market within which to trade at any given turn. There will always be leftovers; the leftovers of the anthropocene and the leftovers of any activism in artistic action are still relevant and attended to. A world created new at every moment is not one without a past. Care for the past without ossifying its tendencies means the ability to think immanently as attentive care for the present and its infinite relations.

The strangest thing about our contemporary need for art and activism is that it does advocate a persistent subject/object, us/them diachrony. While anthropocentric subjects, the parasites whose taking is vindicated by their human exceptional rhetoric, always have within them molecules of ahuman despotism, ahuman practices strive to slough off anthropocentrism, or at least only use anthropocentric privilege to fight against human exceptionalism. This shows our inherent entanglement. Ahumanism resists the vaguely eugenic whiff of being considered evolutionary, but I am drawn for two reasons to invoke the memento mori in the Crypt of the Cappuccini at Santa Maria della Concezione in Barberini populated by the mummies, bones and robed skeletons of the Cappuccini Monks who announce, 'What you are now, we once were, what we are now, you shall be.' First, the inevitability of death speaks to me of a belief in the inevitability of the death of the anthropocene (there are optimistic and pessimistic manifestation possibilities for these deaths; I will discuss what they may look like). Second, because the ahuman does not impose a template of what the new or next human will be, belief in the powers of activism and art commit continued hope in the capacity for affective change in unpredictable and often imperceptible ways. There is no wholesale us or them. The entanglement itself goes both ways. Much as we would love to state we do not want to benefit from human exceptionalism we do unless we self immolate. The moment of the memento mori of the Cappuccini is the decisive moment of immanence where we can attend to both expressivity and affectivity, the activism of all everyday activity as a form of art in the face of these mummified monks whose effulgent corruption is its own form of the art of the death of the human as an opening of the world. Entanglement between ahuman and anthropocentric practices resonates with the continued entanglement between subject and object, self and world. The question for art and activism is how to give, how to reciprocate, without balance or measure, how to set anthropocentrism on fire and configure the pyre as that of a phoenix rather than a martyr.

Wanting to maintain activism in a world beyond identity politics, especially that which self serves, involves a considerable amount of imagination. It requires forming alliances with unlikely participants, Deleuze and Guattari's unnatural participations without filiation. It involves traversing territories not entirely demarcated, and the act of traversal that refutes the borders takes precedence over the borders, the ablation of which is itself an act of art. Kristeva (1991) marks this self estrangement as critical to breaking down notions of foreignness. Braidotti (2010) points out that traditional understandings of chaos, via Hegelian (then Lacanian and Derridean) Western metaphysics, is a key diversion from the Kristevan, Deleuzio-Guattarian and Spinozist definitions of chaos as virtual potential. For Kristeva, the subject is fearful of the foreigner within such an antagonistic polar structure because, as contemporary media will testify, the foreigner brings chaos within this dialectic understanding, trailing the chaos from which they flee. What is largely ignored is that the chaos of the homeland of the refugee is one instituted by capitalist war patterns of territorialization, whether it be a war which profits from arming government or insurgents or a war against the environment for profit. The human of colour and the furred, fanged and winged person are all perceived as chaotic because they are victims of Western capital remapping. This form of perceiving the wild nonhuman or barely human is representation as a form of violence devoid of imagination and entirely without art. Covertly, Kristeva says of the capacity of art to revolutionize:

> In his [sic] work the artist performs the 'right' kind of violence: by appropriating what is outside of him he achieves a balance between the self and the world … the artist's role is not to make a faithful copy of reality, but to shape our attitude towards reality. This balance, this harmony, this genuine act of revolt is not about domination or concealment but about the interstice, about appropriating and *being possessed*, about the resonance between self and world. (2002: 122, my emphasis)

Kristeva's definition of self (artist or otherwise) is 'permanent questioning, of transformation, change, an endless probing of appearances' (2002: 120). While it may seem that the popular media obliquely operates a similar artistic practice in reporting the 'news', they adamantly claim to be reporting reality under the guise of neutral objectivity while shaping a narrative whose evil is not in its misinformation or rhetoric but in its claimed relationship with truth. There is truth to be found in the post-truth era but not in the media. Truth finds illumination through perceptions in the dark, alternative modes and aspects, baroque flashes and glimpses that train us to see differently at every turn, the art-perception and art-creation that occurs in the interstice, the in-between. Art and activism working as co-emergent rupture dialectic metaphysical fear of chaos by acknowledging chaos as that which has not yet been atrophied by signification. For revolution through activism as artistic practice, we are compelled to see that chaos within everything, otherwise we are doomed to the despair the world media feeds us in its own perverted mode of artistic information transmission. The self should be first to go for three interdependent reasons: (1) self-interest is not enough (and not ethical) for activism; (2) the self cannot perceive art because perception has been pre-ordained before an encounter with an issue or an other; and (3) the self as its own pre-ordained subjectivization has its past and future territorialized, so its capacity for activism is limited. Kristeva states that the artist must be possessed, and indeed they must, by occulture spirits and demons perhaps, by the other they can never know perhaps, by the simple drive to not self-sustain and yet, remaining alive, drives them effervescing and asking 'how can I do?'

Art makes us unthink the world we know, and activism makes us think an unknowable world in which we believe but which we may never see (and where the sketch of this new world is a tactical proposal only, never a utopia or goal). The constant in both is metamorphic mobility without a singular disappearing point that differentiates activism and art from the hypermobility of semiocapitalism that is also constantly changing but consistent in its final aim of increment. Posthuman subjectivity decries the celebrity of the artist for the queer weirdness of the therian ahuman (those who identify as nonhuman and who embraces the fae, vampire and werewolf as readily as the mammal or reptile in spite of the etymology of the word), against the nihilistic embrace of the weird that existential-crisis-driven men are turning towards in their embrace of world where the inconsequentiality of man is absolute (the so-called turn to the 'weird'). We are still unsure of the status of the therian in identity politics – other non-natal birth ascriptions are already fraught enough – but their adamantly fictional status is something artistic and baroque in its refusal at revelation we can deploy as activists in our equally baroque activist practices. As art, they are beyond all-or-nothing successes; activism is not a war campaign to win or lose. That kind of structure belongs in a dialectic. Like being vegan, the hardest thing about being an activist (and possibly an artist) is not found in the practice itself but in the eye-rolling from the anthropocentric who tirelessly asks, 'But what about ...?' in order to find flaws in a practice that, if not perceived as perfectable, can only be understood anthropocentrically as defunct. The anthropocentric invests all the affects of both into the being, while the vegan, the activist, the therian, the covetous of revolt cares only about the perturbation of the clinamen, the rupture, the interstice, about being possessed at the expense of self – overrated, overvalued. Imagining being an acting subject with other acting subjects without being able to imagine the subject who acts and the outcome of the action as valid only if won or lost is the foundation of activism and what keeps it supple. This manifesto advocates death in many ways and the death of the subject who retains the capacity to act is a crucial moment in acknowledging the powers of every organism, no matter how limited. When our signification is forsaken, we must rely on our imagination, to live and to die, and this makes artists of us all. So the question is, At every moment, with every encounter, how will we imagine the world?

3

Interregnum

The first part of *The Ahuman Manifesto* has demarcated problems with anthropocentric structures and reasons why these are detrimental to biogea. The following two chapters are experimental offerings as to practical activisms which could be mediated in order to create Ahuman trajectories as implemental experiments, implemental because they are pragmatic while still accessing the art element of activism, and experiments because while being suggestions for implementation of practices, they are only suggestions and not demands or demarcations, which are the exclusive domain of Ahuman practice. They are collations of history, aesthetics, materiality and rituals delivered from their anthropocentric exclusivity in an attempt to produce loose guides for how we can act Ahuman and exploit the many Ahuman practices contemporary relations with art and activism encourage. Specifically, the two chapters deal with occulture and death activism as escape routes from anthropocentrism but that assist us in remaining within, of and for biogea.

Occulture is the contemporary world of occult practice which embraces a bricolage of historical, fictional, religious and spiritual trajectories to create rituals that replace institutes of belief such as religion, traditional family, state, educational institute, economic systems and even government. It, like art and activism, is an unlimited world of imagination and creative disrespect for epistemes and so does not create hierarchies of truth based on myth or materiality, law or science. It indulges in faith and hope in the same way activism as artistic practice do, while knowing itself to always be true only to the extent it acknowledges the lived material realities of organisms and individuals, and untrue in that it engages fiction to catalyse Ahuman becomings. The history of 'man' – from ancient religions to modern fictional universes – are all invoked equally while being delivered from their relationship with power and thus with their anthropocentric signifying purposes. Primarily encouraged by a new embrace of the trinity of anti-religion against all fundamentalism of any kind, of biogea as the primary purpose of life and of the redemption of the image of the witch representing all disruptive women and outsiders, contemporary occulture is vast and expansive. My exploration, while mentioning occulture's expansiveness, including its machismic and right-wing factions, creates a new adaptation of chaos magick practice that aligns/allies itself explicitly with the history of women, minorities and nonhuman animals in Western pre- and Christian religions as well as the rising interest in various occult areas in addition to chaos magick, such as Luciferianism, modern witchcraft and the embrace of the inconsequentiality of the human in the pantheonic fiction of H. P. Lovecraft and the demonic sorcery of Deleuze and Guattari. What my exploration of occulture also seeks to emphasize is the redundancy (albeit dangerous) of the far-right, neo-Nazi, 'kek' assimilation of occultism. That version is driven by the futility of the majoritarian when privilege is denied (considering it was never deserved) and is, in its fascism, utterly lacking in imagination, basing its power on empty symbols designed to intimidate and destroy. These techniques are entirely at odds with the creative fecundity of Ahuman occulture as an effulgent enchantment rather than a destructive strategy of reintegrating an absurdly romanticized mythical great past. I could mention the rise of indigenous animism, especially as animism has played a strong role in Western chaos via Austin Osman Spare; however, I do not think I could give it the nuanced attention others can. Occulture appeals to Ahumanism because of this antithetical history, because it is about misuse as much as use, because it queers the tools available to it and because it taps into new paradigms of value that resist phallocratic capitalist hierarchies. And, of course, because it is fascinating, populated by monsters and angels, demons and hybrids, encouraging and emphasizing the importance of being unlike the other in ethical becomings, in activisms and ultimately unlike the human in order to destroy the anthropocene.

Death activism, like occulture, involves practices that privilege the end of self – as individual and as species. Death activism is not suicidal (though they can include personal and assisted suicide as forms of activism) because death is an imaginative, pro-ethical activist technique to end the human and open the world rather than the human's lamentable end as the end of the world, so while the traditional use of suicide remains relevant, I do not see the capacity for suicide of a species as a tenable expression due to the emphasis on absence. Death practices are anthropomorphically absenting, but for the earth and its nonhuman occupants, they are richly liberating. Death practices in this manifesto include the address of the death of the nonhuman other as being of equal value as the death of a human,

human extinction/antinatalism as the most plausible and easiest activism towards the survival of the earth, imaginative practices involving human corpses so that we/they may become the host upon which the other feeds rather than humans remaining the eternal parasite. Death activism is emphatically vitalistic. It is not a cult of death in the same way the war machine, the capitalism machine, religious and political terrorism or the industrialized genocide of humans and nonhumans see death as a means to an end that elevates the murderer. Death activism values the other, the left behind as a left be as a result of the death of the self and the human species. It also gifts the self their own life through advocating greater control of and access to one's own death as an inherent right rather than extension of life at all costs, including the cost of living as a state of suffering. Like occulture's inconsequentiality of the human being liberating rather than existentially horrifying, death activism is death offering optimism and an opportunity for imaginative practices of deceleration and the care that it will involve for the earth and all of its occupants.

Occulture and death activism share with the previous chapters an advocacy of the cessation of self, whether through the possession of self that Kristeva advocates that all artists must undergo, or the actual end of self that Bifo sees as increasingly impossible in contemporary capitalism. They resonate a memory of identity by tapping into and privileging minoritarian incarnations but lose nothing through giving up on new modes of reification towards an impossible goal of equality with the anthropocentric majoritarian. Like activism, occulture and death activism are first and foremost about creating relations with an indefinable, often unthinkable or non-present other. Hope and faith come about through identifying the potential affects rather than the beneficiaries of these activisms. The chapters may read as strange, definitely experimental, likely engaging in concepts that may seem extreme, especially as we live in a world that still ignores mass death and that has high suicide rates and gender-based murder. But death is the most banal inevitability; it is in its patterns that injustice is found. Similarly, the world is driven in various ways by manifold religious fundamentalisms – fictions posing as truths that lead to material and real actions and outcomes, both violent and benevolent. Occulture is another way to think affective materializations through the joy of fiction acknowledged as such.

4

Occulture

Secular spirituality

Ahuman activism deals with the institutional signifying paradigms that both constitute and perpetuate anthropocentrism. Arguably the oldest is religion, and in contemporary times we see a rise of what I would term old-fashioned (fundamentalist, absolute) religious thought and oppression, in diverse countries and cultures. Like faith and hope in activism, faith and hope in religion are founded on a belief. However, unlike faith and hope in activism, the belief in religion is preceded by two issues – the supremacy (and verisimilitude) of man on earth with God(s) in heaven, and extended from this belief both dominion over earth and the denial of death through a promised afterlife. What many religions share with the most ubiquitous modern secular religion of capitalism is a narrative of strive hard, do well and you shall be rewarded, which is, of course, a monumentally ludicrous myth. Many religions also impose harsh arbitrary subject norms, in addition to dominion over nonhumans claiming a divine right over women, racial others, non-heteronormative sexualities and so forth.

I could cite myriad anthropological and sociological examples (such as Weber, especially in his connection between Christianity and capitalism), and for each there is likely an exception. Additionally, as I have already stated, the tenets of religion in their judiciary claims are not extricated from science or state. This would create an enormous diversion, so I offer sketched generalizations as religious 'tendencies'. The edicts and licit and illicit rules of many religions result in morality, a potestas-driven regime, emphasizing their resonance with the Oedipal family, with hierarchies of State, and thus showing anthropocentric institutions in general as founded on a religiosity no matter their relationship with an imagined being or beings. What I hope to do here is offer just one alternative paradigm of belief which involves (and invokes) practices that shatter this hierarchy and can produce the end of the self-serving/God-serving subject that oppresses, by creating suggestions for practices which embrace hitherto aberrant elements of religion – the feminine, the animal, the demonic, the multiple, the fluid – and that also attend to the rising interest in non-traditional spiritual rituals and practices across the world but as antagonistic to a nostalgic right-wing return to tradition seen not only in neo-fascist occultism but also recent manifesti, from Norway to New Zealand. Ahuman occulture is an entirely adaptable creative mode of activism – individual and collective, DIY, anti-hierarchical and absolutely driven by commitment to and compassion for alterity.

This chapter invokes the trend rising from the 1960s and increasing today of what is now known as 'occulture' – a reimagining and embracing of a decidedly fabulated form of spirituality. Its roots lie as far back as the tenth century in the sects of Catharism and

Manichaeism which saw the world and all material reality as satanic because materiality stood in opposition to the ethereal eternity of God. It has also seen rises in the Renaissance through Enochian magic, in the early Romantics with Blake, Coleridge and Swedenborg, and has found popularity with late Romantics who were members of the Golden Dawn as well as more surprising inspirations such as those coming from reinterpretations of Satan from Milton's opus *Paradise Lost*, including Victorian feminist philosophers and theorists. Theosophical and Thelemic teachings of the early twentieth century similarly influenced all manner of left, right, feminist and traditional thinkers, writers and artists showing the adaptability of occult schools even in their most rigid and systematic forms. But the pop explosion of contemporary occulture can be seen as part of the general counterculture embrace of difference, where the clandestine nature of occult practice gave way to garish performativity that seemed to merge the parlour room spectacle of superstition driven false magic with the more serious commitment to seeing beyond traditional Judaeo-Christian perception in magick (I use Aleister Crowley's spelling to demarcate this difference). Differentiating itself from the fetishistic assimilation and cultural appropriation of new-ageism, occulture is a bricolage of fin-de-siècle magick, apocryphal esoterica, chaos theory from physics to magick practice, carnivalesque Luciferianism as a foil to the anthropocene, popular film, music and art, and it limits itself by nothing, excluding nothing. Within my context, occulture is defined rudimentarily as an unbound set of practices driven by beliefs that would be considered traditionally non-religious (chaos magick, Thelema), pseudo-Judaeo-Christian (Theosophics, Golden Dawn) pre-religious (paganism, Celtic, Norse and other pre-Christian beliefs), anti-religious (Satanism, Luciferianism) and what I would loosely term fabulative because ideas and entities formerly deployed under the rubric of superstition are engaged for magickal purposes (vampires, therians, Necronomic Ancient Ones and Elder Gods, even Pantheonic gods and pre-Greco-Roman deities). These are only a few of the most visible drivers, and they are not necessarily discrete from one another in occulture. In terms of practice, each personal or collective emergence of occult practice will differ, as will the level of identification and commitment of the individuals and collectives. Like all assimilated movements, occulture has been rebranded and marketed as much as any other social movement, but it remains borderless and unverifiable, so while in-fighting may see cries of 'You're not doing it right' or 'You're not a real x practitioner', all that is really needed in contemporary occulture to practice is a little (or a lot of) reading and a desire to do and think via alternative perceptions to what are currently available. For my own understanding and use of occulture, this aspect especially is crucial. The media love to tell us of celebrities turning to occult gurus to embrace the next or newest 'obscure' (i.e. entirely mainstream if not tediously boring) branch of Western esotericism. Occulture requires no guru beyond self-inspiration, although communities of occultists are invaluable for sharing and disseminating knowledge, as my own experience as a London occultist testifies. Power, however, especially power that forms hierarchies, is not part of an ahuman embrace of occulture, and perhaps this is where the adept reader will see what is obvious while the non-occultist may be surprised. Most representations of the occult, of practice and of well-known occultists see any practice as one for power – the satanic meglomaniac, the vengeful witch, the endlessly hungry vampire or therian, all of which take alone without giving (much more like the far scarier capitalist than the occultist). Occult practice in everyday life does not follow this rather glamorous and simpler causal path. Occulture is about producing affects which alter modes of behaviour and thought in the practitioner and thereby altering the practitioner's monadic expression and navigation of the world. Frighteningly this may be why we find occult books next to self-help hack psychology books in the larger-chain stores. Occulture is the opposite of the cult of ego that self-help produces. It refines the ego towards nothingness and refutes the consumerist myth of integrated completeness towards which self-help aspires. It is becoming-imperceptible and endlessly metamorphic. Transcendental subjectivity has no place in occulture unless to transcend anthropocentrism perhaps. If there is an absolute to be reached (which there is not) it would be protean zero. As becomes evident, contradictions abound. For ahuman purposes, occulture is a way to maintain words commonly associated with religious institutes – belief, hope, faith – that we need to change this world without any thought of the phantasmatic promised next world. It shares much with the role and purpose of science fiction, horror and fantasy literature, art and film in this sense. It is neither true nor untrue but only useful in changing the way we think and perceive in order to change a world with which we are increasingly becoming despairing. Returning to the spectre of power, while not wishing to divide occulture into a set of binaries that map it onto established isomorphic patterns, I will say a word about what I would see as two common tendencies in occult practice as they are important in understanding that occulture can be a highly anthropocentric practice even while deploying other-worldy methodology – results-based and immersive practitioner. The almost carnivalesque figures of the evil satanic priest or witch performing a basic ritual to gain a clear objective is a media favourite because it highly simplifies both the occult icon and the complexity of occult practice. Occult practice in the twenty-first century does tend to fall into two continuation categories of established traditions, no matter what the order (or disorder). Some occultists do perform rituals only for self-oriented results, whether these be the stereotypical wealth, fame, sex, revenge or even happiness and other abstract semiocapitalist-based moods which cease desire. These finite demarcated forms of ritual are not very reliable and they tend to insinuate an absolute belief in occultism that resonates with established formal religions that utilize prayer or confession for results. The vast majority of occulture is not interested in this immediate gratification form of results-based magick, whether because it is often unsuccessful or ultimately fundamentalist. The manifestation of power for the immersive practitioner defines power in the more Foucauldian sense of *puissance*, force or Spinoza's potentia, expressivity, unbound desire before and beyond an object and in excess of self. Loss of self is a key aspect of occulture's pleasure, in order to remake the self and remake the world, because the patterns within our neural, social and environmental networks are so deeply trodden it takes a form (sometimes many forms) of death to reinvigorate them, seen, for example, in death-posture rituals in chaos magick. This kind of occulture is always group work, whether it accesses the collective selves within the one, evincing the practitioner as a kind of schizo-mage, or work in groups, covens, orders which resist hierarchy. Occulture seeks to change perception, to change the world, when the current modes of perception, activism and creativity may feel as if they are not doing enough or are not adapting as well as they could. It is an alternative way to find inspiration, neither better nor worse than any other. While attending to the former more stereotypical understanding of occultism, the ahuman welcome of occulture works with the latter.

Occulture has aligned itself with the emptying of material meaning and end of subjectivity insinuating end of purposefulness of life of object-oriented ontology that makes demands of the object/other, and speculative realism, as well as a vitalistic queer ecosophical practice. What can occulture offer ahuman theory between the death drive of, for example, Islamic State or the white male sniper, and the annihilation of liberty in Fundamental Christianity as a neither-neither thinking of something beyond the tension between religion, rights and arid scientific essentialism? Nietzsche associates the valuation of religion with nihilism and decadence in *The Anti-Christ* (2005: 6), stating that religion is a negation of reality (2005: 25). For Nietzsche, the jubilance of the material Jesus, whom I could call an activist, is entirely estranged from religious signifying edicts of Christianity. It is difficult to suggest what drives contemporary occulture beyond an immediate coalescence of dissatisfaction merged with a drive for creativity that is materially affective without being true or false, good or evil. This continues the many passages ahumanism takes us through where often something which is seen as an absence or negation (abolition, antinatalism and, here, atheism or, more correctly, antitheism) results not in negative emptiness but a voluminously creative space that demands unique and singular practices of remodelling the world temporarily and tactically in order to express redistribution of powers and affects.

Popular culture, particularly in the United States, has since the acid luridity of the pop art wave, adored both the occult and monsters, which in this chapter will be intimately co-emergent. Comics and television have given consumers wizards and witches, both other-worldy and teenaged high school or housewife, and these have found companionship with vampires, werewolves and a menagerie of monsters. Currently, the claim of an occult renaissance in popular culture is no more than the result of a reattention to a kind of punk DIY turn to spirituality when both all organized religions and governments are alienating, fascist, a mess or all three. Occulture as I will present it as an ahuman practice is disorganized organizational DIY practice that is a means by which we monsters live in the spaces between the organizations that currently threaten to fail us. While occulture has never gone away, so a claim to a renaissance is moot, it does seem to be out and proud more so during times of tightened so-called moral, normative and limiting regimes, especially for outsiders and minoritarians, and for this reason I claim it is an inherently queer form of spirituality. This demarcates what I term occulture from the more traditionally structured occult lodges and orders which follow the ecclesiastic practices of hierarchy, leader (usually always white heterosexual or power-driven sexual male, concealed or otherwise), lodge members, practices built on incremental increases in power leading to increase in order rank and so forth, and usually those adopted by neo-fascist movements. Some of the magickal practices I will discuss maintain order structures, such as the Crowley-based

Thelemic order the Ordo Templi Orientis (O.O.O., but I will use the word Thelema so as not to confuse the order with the philosophical object-oriented ontology [OOO]) and chaos magick's Illuminates of Thanateros (I.O.T.). Even these orders are clear that membership and lodge practice is not inherent to the beliefs. Occulture invokes (literally) the reimagining of the term 'belief' because occulture defies beliefs as set, as preceding subject or practice (so there is no subject and the practice must be designed for each purpose), and occulture has the strange and dubious relationship with belief in that it believes in something whose truth or falsity is irrelevant. Its potential affectivity and capacity to change perception is all that matters. After all, the panacea placebo of transubstantiation to the Catholic taking communion can, to the outsider, be perceived as a ritual of institutionalized cannibalism and vampirism. In this way, occulture occupies an odd position, or at least decidedly queer, in that it queers the truth through belief in the blatantly untrue or disprovable. Humans and all other affected organisms are in a world where the truth has been lost through outright lying, misreporting or concealment via mass, social and governmental media. The last decade especially has seen a desire for a return to a form of truth in a so-called post-truth age. While initially this may seem to be a backlash against postmodernity's death of truth, the return to truth aligns more with a return to attentiveness to the reality of the multiple truths that the truths of the few ablate. Postmodernity's death of truth proliferated truths rather than implementing only falsity. Posthumanism's truth proliferated those who could both enunciate and access truth by multiplying the validity of experiences which did not conform to dominant homogenous grand truth narratives, both historical and scientific. Ahuman's relationship with truth is driven by metamorphosing despair into imagination by taking all those multiple actual experiential truths – what happened, what is happening, to whom, by whom, how – and exploiting their contingency to change the world, enhancing the truths that are ethically beneficial (Spinoza's 'joy'), diminishing those which are detrimental (Spinoza's 'pain'). Ahumanism does not judge truth via value, so it is postcapitalist – one truth is no better than another if the truths are materially real to those who experience them. It does not judge falsity by its fictionality – just because something is false it does not diminish its capacity to affect perception, action and the world. Artists have always attended to the power of falsity without judgement. Occulture is a form of spiritual artistic practice because it uses acknowledged falsity, fiction and fabulation, coupled with belief as a commitment to attending to changing contemporary truthful scenarios by utilizing a weird toolkit of somewhat rigid but nonetheless queerly bendy practices in order to maintain a hope in this world.

A brief history of occulture; Witches, monsters and queerdos

What is occult practice? As a proviso, this chapter deals with only the adoption of Western occult practice (and selectively at that). I will not be addressing any non-European-based magickal practices or traditions because that is not for me to do, and ethical occult practice should avoid fetishistic appropriation at all costs. Contemporary occulture is fetishistic appropriation to an extent, of ancient and seriously adhered-to traditions, but to do this for non-Western practices is not appropriate (keeping in mind many of the traditions I will discuss had a considerable amount of their own appropriation, some of which was encouraged by the indigenous practitioners, but more on this later). Readers of this manifesto of course may be thorough adepts at occult practices or they may think occultism burned with the last European witches, and that Crowley, modern Satanism and witchcraft belong to the realm of carnival hacks, cult gurus and marketing trends. Both are the case. I am not seeking to validate occulture for contemporary times, but I am in the fortunate position of finding myself in a crossroad (of course, the most highly charged of magickal places where criminals and witches hang) of European magickal traditions of the nineteenth and twentieth centuries, feminist practices of subversion, queer experiments in performative practices which put the body on the line, and the rise of so-called extreme anti-religion in places like Scandinavia, while on the other side of the Bosporus my queer Turkish academic colleagues are being expelled and exiled and entire populations are being actually demonized by their own countries and fundamentalist religious stricture. Meanwhile, arguably the most fundamentalist religious country in the world, the United States, the same one which also claims to be the most free, has a messianic leader whose Money God seems on his side. All the while the rise of the right is occurring in ways we have not witnessed since the 1930s. Extreme times call for extreme imagination, which can be understood as hope, as compassion, as extreme alterity, all of which directly challenge the extreme right as a repetition of a phantasmatic lost pattern, which is an excuse for imposing violence and power. If the United States and other religious fundamentalist countries of any religion see themselves as God's people, all I can say is bring on the Antichrist and End of Days. To the Cathars and Manichaeans, all material reality was satanic, so movements such as material feminism and real-life politics are deemed satanic already. Material reality, acknowledgement of the physical affects of violence and power, celebration of the actual liberty of bodies seem to be distasteful to the abstraction of lives, bodies and singularities of relations of difference that fundamental religion, right-wing politics and media, and capitalism enforces. Valuing all material incarnations of life, especially all as collectives of difference, refuses to reduce organisms to units of use or statistics in comparison to the abstract transcendental God of currency/semiocapitalism. Fear of End of Days by religion has a long narrative tendency to follow the rise of minoritarians in claiming their rights. The end of feudalism, the rise of feminism, the abolition of slavery, queer dismantling of heteronormativity have all led to various versions of cries of 'burn them at the stake ... in the name of God'. Global politics is now seeing legislation follow this cry and some legal 'reforms' are astonishingly backward in wanting to put the outsider back where they belong. The clearest example is found in the bodies of women, who are now facing returns to pre-1960s reproductive legislation denying access to abortion and contraception. The rise of sexual slavery globally and the persistence of the 'she asked for it' rhetoric in rape and assault trials (if indeed they come to trial) as well as female child marriage, female genital mutilation and other practices that seek to 'tame' wild women show that the fear of the witch has never gone away. Witch is nothing more here than a woman who seeks agency over her own body and drives. From a post-identity perspective, this extends to any bodies who do not 'pass' – current trans* legislations of self-identification versus legal recognition, people of colour always more scrutinized for their 'wild' appetites and behaviours, and, of course, any nonhuman body that is made to behave or be tamed. Perversely (and not the good kind of perversion) male predators from extreme kek men's rights activists to privileged frat boys are claiming they are the victim of witch hunts, mistaking truth as reality for their truth that only their perception of having a right to the world's bodies to do with as they wish is viable. This resonates with human exceptionalism. Taming nature and exploiting nonhuman bodies, destroying those that do not behave, is a classic witch-burning exercise. If we cannot use them, we shall destroy them. What we won't do is allow them ownership over their own bodies, capacities for expression and freedoms.

But this chapter seeks to explore the positives. We already know about the Witchfinder General that is anthropophallologocentric culture. What we want to know is how to fight it without having to resort to its tools and its terms. There have always been witches, whether seen as positive or negative. At the most basic level, witchcraft takes non-verifiable acts of sorcery to evoke alterations in patterns of habit, tendencies of practice and demands change. Historically, witchcraft and sorcery were embraced and maligned. The figure of the witch and the somewhat clandestine (although spectacle can be powerful) nature of the practice, coupled with a sense of transgression is what has remained. So this 'history' is only a history of what we have now and how we use it. The history of modern occulture is as diverse as the welcoming of Hecate, Erishkigal, Inanna, Medea, ancient female sorcerers from Sumeria, Babylonia, Mesopotamia and Greece whom the Reformation transformed into icons of evil. It includes Mary Wollstonecraft's (1975) effulgent critique of women's relegation as either object to be adored or subject to be despised and thus her alignment with Milton's Satan more than God or Eve. It forms the foundation of those women in Victorian literature who don't care to be adored and who lean towards the satanic hero over the God-fearing patriarch or science-seeking suitor, from Jane Eyre's selection of a deformed Rochester over St John (though had she met Bertha Mason, we know she would have gone to her instead), to Lucy Westenra preferring death and Dracula to any Victorian doctors. It is seen in literature, in art and in music. It memorializes Ida Craddock, the theosophist with an angel 'bridegroom' who took her own life in 1902 rather than go to jail for circulation of obscene literature, literature that simply taught women how to enjoy non-procreative sex with husbands and celestial lovers. It revisits the horrors of the witch trials and what feminism can do with enchantment in the works of Silvia Federici (2004, 2018) and Barbara Ehrenreich and Deirdre English (2010). It exists in contemporary rereadings of apocryphal biblical tales of the Watchers in the *Book of Enoch* (Charles 2003) who fell from heaven to teach knowledge to the daughters of men (but showed zero interest in said men). None of these are interested in truth or falsity, though they are aware of the power of fiction and alternative narratives. Occulture is not modern, superstitious hangovers. It is neither naive nor delusional, and it does not seek to replace religion or atheism. It is welcoming the repressed underside of religious practice (indivisible for millenia from artistic practice) where women, minorities and resistors incandesce and offer alternative creative catalysts for the stale, barren wasteland of the three spiritual options we currently have: organized religion, capitalism and pop fetishistic new-age spiritual hokum. All of these are clearly versions of semiocapitalism because all seek to reap a profit, fiscal and ideological. DIY occulture has nothing to sell. Its irreverent and often shameless bricolage of any and every religious tradition makes it slippery and mucosal, tentacular and elusive, personal, political and terrifying to the dominant but deeply comforting to the practitioner's opportunities for belief in change. It is the strange world where Haraway's Chthulucene (2016) tentacles meet Lovecraft's Cthulhu Mythos (bedfellows who would despise each other), because Haraway cannot deny the inspiration from Lovecraft, no matter how deplorably racist and sexist, and Lovecraft cannot deny the inspiration from feminism, where the human is perceived as so inconsequential that only becoming-monster and imperceptible with the cosmos can save one's existence. It is queer bodies desiring the demonic evocations offered in post-reformation occult magick such as Eliphas Levi (1969, 2001) and Regis's *The Lesser Key of Solomon* (1995), for we are lesser, demonic and proudly so. It is identity politics identifying with non-identities, merging with monsters. For feminism, and attending to my own initial inspiration towards making unnatural participations, as Deleuze and Guattari would call them, with sorcerers, it is cunt chaos. Occultures's intimacy with esoteric practice has a varied heritage spanning Thelema, Luciferian Satanism and chaos magick. Like the music and the artwork associated with some more phallic examples of antithetical Satanism or anti-religious occulture, however, the occulture aligned with modern Satanism, Lodge mentality, chaotic death orders such as The Order of the Nine Angles and Black Metal has usually been a machismic and nationalistic, if not fascist, affair. Occult practices often tend towards the nihilistic or antithetical, devoid of politics or openly right wing and ultimately exhibiting an attraction to the void as a nothing. But just because human lives are meaningless it does not mean we cannot create ecosophically jubilant affects with them.

Cunnus chaosium: Minoritarian magick

Against this destructive-towards-nothingness void mentality of some of the more phallocratic, right-wing and nostalgic adaptations of left-hand path occulture, I wish to offer a void that is voluminous and a set of paradigmatic working tools that are highly adaptive and which privilege the very tenets that the phallic nationalist adaptations of occulture are both terrified of and seek to destroy – the feminine (or more precisely the vulvic), the animal, the hybrid, submission (as compassion), loss of identity and loss of self. This section traces some historical paradigms that assist in understanding why the cunt has been deemed antithetical toward anthropocentrism, particularly phallocentrism. Some of this research is over a decade old but when submitted was deemed vulgar. When a far more respectable and less occult (i.e. *no* occult) version of a mere sketch of these ideas was published in 2010 (MacCormack 2010), the journal *New Formations* demanded that I change the word cunt to vulva. What the following section offers is a cunt working – practical entities and genealogies which, while feminist because they are cunt forms, are inherently queer and not necessarily human because they show an absolute disregard for phallic and anthropocentric paradigms while emphasizing how certain forms and forces affiliated with the feminine, the nonhuman animal, the monster and the aberrant or abject have formed the foundation of so-called 'left-hand path' or 'black' magick. The reader is invited to do with them what thou will.

A renaissance in chaos magick is occurring among feminist and queer occultists that shares in the romance for the void but rather than spiralling into it wants to invoke the void and its myriad monsters into this world to change the contemporary patterns of tedious capitalist and masculine heteronormative art, music and culture. I have termed this 'cunt chaos'. This system is based on the basic tenets of chaos magick, inspired primarily by the queer work of Chaos auteur Phil Hine (1993, 2004) and his use of H. P. Lovecraft, mingled with the enticing perversions of Irigaray's work on sex with angels (1992) and Charles's version of *The Book of Enoch*, augmented by Craddock's heavenly bridegroom celestiosexual feminism (2017). (Sadly, female chaos authors are rare, with the exception perhaps of the practical work of Jaq D. Hawkins [1996].) What all these mystical practices share is a belonging to the void wherein monsters dwell and a drive to consummate with these monsters to produce infernal and aberrant offspring – art, music, writing, action and activism – that is as creative as nihilistic theory but more baroque and voluminous. Thus, this form of occulture also partakes of teratology which influences contemporary queer and feminist practices, and all theories addressing those bodies who do not 'pass'. Chaos magick is more a way of perceiving the world differently than a set belief. It prefers the multiple and fractal over single modes of understanding; it welcomes the metamorphic and transformative rather than seeking unified fixed identity; it demands that we unthink everything we thought we knew. The multiple and metamorphic nature of chaos thinking shares much with contemporary feminist concerns. While various occulture streams are populated with posturing men seeking fame through an atrophied idolized persona, feminist emergences are always, like Satan, legion, for we are many. The succubus, the witch, the daughters of men to whom the Watchers came to teach us the ways of angels, the Fallen Eve, the sanguine Lilith. In the United States, this has resulted in Luciferian feminists actually challenging misogynist laws by claiming religious protection (see the Missouri Abortion Reform challenge by The Satanic Temple, Campbell 2018).

In Europe, the rise of feminist occultists has been simultaneous with that of renewed rigour in both academic feminist occultism and occult queer art practices. They share what I call the four angles of cunt chaos technologies: (1) Technologies of Alterity – the feminine, the queer, multiplicity, chaosium; (2) Technologies of Abstraction – ritual without capital; (3) Technologies of Ecstasy – cacodaemonic copulation; and (4) Technologies of Watchers/Fallen Angels – interstitial, ambiguous, without genesis or destination. Cunt chaos refuses a single standpoint or set of rules, defying the tendency especially in satanic Black Metal to be verified as 'true' – in Aleister Crowley's pseudo-Nietzschean lesson in *Magick without Tears* (1991), nothing is true, everything is permitted. Like many (perhaps even most) writers of seminal occult works of each era, Crowley and Lovecraft are marred by frequent misogynist and racist rants that, also like many of the driving forces of carnival hierarchical Luciferian lodges, Black Metal and other contemporary examples of occulture, say more about the navigation of the individual with the uniting themes of their human inconsequentiality rather than with a megalomania driven loathing of the other (although let's not rule that out entirely – both Black Metal and neo-occultism include fascist factions). Examples of feminist and queer occulture are not so much rare as more difficult to source, and their drive to change is usually catalysed by the development of a weird world from which they are not alienated but rather with which they feel connected. This differentiates will-driven magick (such as results-based rituals, usually again phallocratically to seek money or sex) with the rise of artistic practical magick that is political and ecosophical. The latter is what I have termed 'cunt chaos'. Clearly, an enormous debt is owed to Irigaray's work on *This Sex Which Is Not One* (Irigaray 1985). I can only call it serendipity that my first encounter with Irigaray's work came not long after reading the entire twenty-four volume occult encyclopaedia set *Man, Myth and Magic* (Cavendish 1970–3) in my Catholic Girls' High School at the age of seventeen, so they are somewhat inseparable unnatural participations in my work.

Cunt chaos finds its kin not in the nationalism of neo-nazi pop occultist symbols or some neo-folk or Black Metal occulture, nor in the desire for money, fame or sex of the results-based practitioners or gurus seeking acolytes, but in kinship with the Lovecraftian monsters of *The Necronomicon* (Simon 1977), who adamantly wear their cuntishness of form and force with Luciferian pride – demons such as Inanna, Ereshkigal and Humwawa who incarnate as viscous, fleshly, mucosal entities with all the features of femininity despised by patriarchy and the new right as abject and horrific. In the entrancing illustrations by Brian Ward for the Chaos bible, Peter Carroll's *Liber Null and Psychonaut* (1987) the portraits of Lovecraft's entities are unmistakably cunt-shaped in infinite incarnations, none phallic, all looking like the mouth of hell toward the chaos of the cosmos that is the power of the cunt unbound. The Necronomicon tells us that The Watchers – the fallen angels of Enoch – come from a race different from that of men and yet different from that of gods. So too do today's occultist feminists. We are not human in this patriarchal world; we do not aspire to being gods because mastery doesn't interest us. The artistic creator of chaos magick, Austin Osman Spare, would call us the 'neither-neither', the space between the spaces between. Driven not by the selfishness borne of meaninglessness in nihilism, or laments of existential angst, but by desire in all of its florid and tenebrous emergences. For cunt chaos, any artistic practice or thought that alters modes of perception is a ritual. Art and writing, both backbones of chaos practice, are deprogramming and creative forms of communion with our pantheon of slimy, tentacled, ephemeral, vulvic gods, who we don't worship but rather with which we engage in cacodemonic copulation to produce progeny designed to tremble the earth and open the Inferno. Far from the clichés of what the media want society to believe feminist queer practices are, stagnant in identity politics, we don't want to be like you. We are not you. We come from chaos and we bring chaos. We are made of chaos as a jubilant force and a void that is teeming. To paraphrase Lovecraft:

> Amidst backgrounds of other planets and systems and galaxies and cosmic continua. Spores of eternal life drifting from world to world, universe to universe, yet all equally self ... self had been annihilated; and yet we – if indeed there could, in view of that utter nullity of individual existence, be such a thing as we – was equally aware of being inconceivable way, a legion of selves. (1999: 526–7)

Practical cunt chaos

Because ahumanism values the reterritorializing potentials of art, ahumans love a ritual. Theatre, music, dramaturgy, chanting and olfactory miasma are no more nor less truthful than activism, but chaos magick in particular utilizes rituals, solitary and collective, to encourage a loss of self. Unlike cults, chaos rituals do not encourage a subscription to a homogenous goal or hierarchically organized transcendental path. They catalyse unthinking established patterns. They encourage openings. Activism requires participating with ideas we have come to believe are impossible but still necessary. Chaos rituals can help access different tactics. Activism requires what Deleuze and Guattari call unnatural participations – non-self-serving goals as well as participating with unlike others – and chaos rituals can help us unlearn ourselves in order to facilitate these unlike assemblages without our atrophied subjects creating fractures. Cunt magick is adamantly anti-phallologocentric while also exploiting the common notions women and nonhuman animals share (because they have been relegated thus). It is, of course, not limited to women, but the paradigms begin with qualities usually ascribed to many alterities. Loss of self in rituals again is not martyrdom, sacrifice or enslavement but becoming-queer with monsters, a repudiation of all taxonomy, making myopic the anthropocentric eye in preference for unique singular monsters, tapping into the field of feminist teratology, albeit here from a pseudo-religious perspective. Importantly, chaos rituals cost nothing except brief amounts of time (increasingly valuable, of course) and so challenge the industrialization of new age and frequently purely 'techniques of the self' practices such as yoga, pilates and other meditations where one pays and which are bourgeois assimilations of ancient ideas. The perhaps surprising influence in chaos of biblical apocrypha and Lovecraft comes from the shared inconsequentiality of the human in both chaos – where to maintain anthropocentric signification makes ritual impossible – and ahuman activism, where loss is a voluminous opening to the universe, albeit this cosmos is not the happy hippy cosmos but a terrifying one occupied with intriguing monsters.

Daemonic invocations access thresholds or, rather, place existence as and at thresholds. Left-hand path magick is that magick which precisely refuses the binarization of the magickal event. It is only black magick when white magick names it such but left-hand path has always been about the very ambiguity between good and evil. These terms are relative and contextual, and like cunts themselves, their form all depends on one's perspective in space and time. The cunt is threshold of internal and external; it is made up of more than one organ – clitoris, labia majora and labia minora, vagina, cervix and the general perineal area – a pineal perinaeum if you like. This multiplicity and inflected folding is contemporary global citizenship of the earth that refuses borders, nation states and fights for free movement while fighting against the phallic raping of the planet and its nonhuman occupants. The cunt is a conceptual gate, just like the gates through which we enter into unnatural worlds and interkingdom, interworld and interspirit alliances in Enochian sex magick and Necronomic chaos magick. Through ritual, we can become demonic cunts – paradigmatically and conceptually. We can think and act like cunts. Cunts belong to the natural order. Their disobedient refusal to be signified and subjectified allies their anti-paradigmatic affects with any flesh that has been deemed wild because natural, or subjugated as part of a social order that denigrates nature. Cunt magick will always include any bodies that are not made in God's image as a refusal to become enslaved to those that resonate with that image, hence the important role of ecosophy in many magickal practices such as neo-paganism, as well as abolitionist animal rights. Cunts, like some nonhuman animals, are hairy and exceed the capacity to be smoothed and made palatable for the phallic eye. Cunt magick is proudly messy, philosophically and materially. As chaos magick is about reprogramming behaviour so narratives of act resonate around experiments and unpredicted results, chaos magick is inherently cuntish. Acts are infinite; even in their repetition there is difference. The burning of sigils shows the voluminous presence of absence, just as the cunt perceived as absent penis does not show lack but rather infinite potential. Like, and through, chaos magick, becoming-cunt is involuted and undone, create a larval sexuality – immature and transformed at every synthesis, which acts not towards a thing but towards its metamorphosis, towards perceiving itself which cannot be perceived, towards the imperceptibility within repetition where all elements within syntheses are dissipated, disoriented and reoriented with each turn, each folding and each alteration in the aspects of involution. Cunts and chaos offer infinity. They never 'know' because they are never things. They are folds, the cunt made of folds of tissue and chaos the folds and pleats of the relation between causality and chance – the exact definition of chaos, although in magick elegant physics and complex or organic chaos, that which develops through the effectuations of affects upon subsequent rituals alters the tenets of the elements involved. If something is made of folds, it can never be known, as a phallus or any 'thing' can be known, described, its function and form reified and its potential immobilized. When things are folded, we have to look around them, and they look different from every angle and every perspective. They are baroque. It is not they but we that have to change and think differently at every angle or perspective. Beyond metaphors of flesh and fold becoming-cunt signifies every part of the flesh, every nerve every tissue mass, every artery, every organ, the unfolded skin as libidinally provocative. In the event of thinking the unthought cunt, skin may be peeled, entrails fondled, parts removed or moved around, corporeal minutia explored and every plane of the body reorganized into a new configuration with new function and meaning. 'The self does not undergo a modification, the self is a modification' (Deleuze 1994: 79). This is apparent of the body whether it be one's own, a conjoining, or the body politic within activist groups. The materiality, exploration, metamorphosis and affects manifest as these many micro and macrocosmic bodies.

Cunnus daemonicus

Becoming implies

> an initial relation of alliance with a demon … There is an entire politics of becomings-animal, as well as a politics of sorcery, which is elaborated in assemblages that are neither those of the family nor of religion nor of the State. Instead they express minoritarian groups, or groups that are oppressed, prohibited, in revolt or always on the fringe of recognized institutions, groups all the more secret for being extrinsic, in other words, anomic. If becoming-animal takes the form of a Temptation, and of monsters aroused in the imagination by the demon, it is because it is accompanied, at its origin as in its undertaking, by a rupture within the central

institutions that have established themselves or seek to become established. (Deleuze and Guattari 1987: 247)

The cunt is a tempting form. Its tempting aspect is traditionally one of the reasons for its danger and the imminent downfall of the (usually majoritarian) tempted. The cunt is also a monster, all the more monstrous for simultaneously being so tempting, evoking the fascination of ambivalence. For all the ways the cunt transgresses and traverses dominant phallic paradigms, it is both prohibited and revolt-ing (in both senses of the word). The cunt, as opposed to the obedient vagina, will not be defined by production (family), chastity (church) or an acceptance of subjugation (state). And it is, above all, an assemblage of folds, organs, elements, textures, tastes and involutions with its disciples. It is, materially and conceptually, a rupture and rupturing. The cunt is a demon – convoked by the sorcerer fascinated with the possible but unknowable futures the cunt offers, tempted by the cunt's seduction against the warnings of family, church, state. But like a demon, the cunt must also be evoked. It will not come unless it is desired, and it cannot materialize unless in the psyche of the sorcerer. The idea of the cunt is the temptation, but its evocation is the demon with which the unholy alliance is formed and the becoming-cunt facilitated.

Many demons in a variety of literature and lore are either cunts or cunt-like. This section will briefly sketch a few examples to show the many resonances occulture has with becoming-cunt, but most demonic forms follow the basic tenets of the cunt as somehow gender ambiguous, as assemblage or fold, as both tempting and dangerous. Against the singularity of the phallus and the majoritarian subject, once again we are reminded, 'My name is Legion: for we are many,' said Satan (Mk 5:9), and so is the cunt and the affinities we form with it.

Leviathan and other cunts

Leviathan is one example of a demonic form becoming-cunt. Leviathan, like cunt, translates from Hebrew as 'that which gathers itself together in folds' (Davidson 1967: 173). Evoking Leviathan welcomes becoming-cunt as a folding with that which folds, offering infinite aspects. Leviathan, even when gathered (tactically unified), is a folding; thus, she transgresses the concept of unity by presenting as a unified folding, or gathering of dimensional aspects. Thomas Hobbes's 1651 *Leviathan* evinces a philosophical emphasis on the breakaway of political logic from the church. Utilizing Leviathan as a metaphor for rupture and transgression of majoritarian power continued the presentation of entering into an affinity with Leviathan as a becoming-cunt. Biblically, Leviathan is a threshold water/land monster, a dragon similar to the crocodile (in the grimoire *The Goetia: The Lesser Key of Solomon* two demons, Sallos and Agares, arrive, when evoked, riding crocodiles) who inhabits the two worlds of land and sea: 'Leviathan the piercing serpent, even leviathan that crooked serpent; ... the dragon that is in the sea' (Isa. 27:1). Isaiah's is an interesting description of an ambivalent penis. A serpent is a clear penile metaphor, but although penile Leviathan does not necessarily behave like a phallus – it is crooked, serpentine (the phallus is rigid, straight and not reticulated or defined by its capacity to move). Per

Faxneld argues for an entire tradition of the tempting satanic serpent as female (2017). Yet Leviathan is still a piercing serpent, resonantly phallic. Job 41:1 offers Leviathan as something internal with parts that extrude 'Canst thou draw out leviathan with an hook? or his tongue with a cord which thou lettest down?'. The Psalms sees Leviathan as suffering because of her own multiplicity, fit for food to a bacchic people: 'Thou brakest the heads of Leviathan in pieces, and gavest him to be meat to the people inhabiting the wilderness' (Ps. 74:14). Leviathan has more than one head. Her seats of logos becomes food, reflecting the proximity of seduction, cannibalism, food, ideology as nourishment, flesh, desire and the creation of thought. Leviathan is contagion through consumption, and her wild disciples become through consumption, resonating with the Maenads and the ultimate fate of Pentheus, whose repudiation of ambiguity led him to be eaten and his head staked. The biblical apocrypha is where we meet Leviathan as a female; 'a female monster named Leviathan, to dwell in the abysses of the ocean, over the fountains of the water ... And I besought the other angel that he should show me the might of those monsters [Leviathan and Behemoth] ... And he said to me: "Thou, son of man, herein thou dost seek to know what is hidden"' (Enoch LX: 7–19, in Charles 2003). Leviathan folds flesh with land with water. She folds as clandestine and to unfold her secrets is to refold one's place with God.

Leviathan is the Hebrew name for the Babylonian goddess Tiamat. Kramer suggests, '[Sumerian] Kur [is] the monstrous creature which at least in a certain sense corresponds to the Babylonian goddess Tiamat, the Hebrew Leviathan and perhaps the Greek Typhon' (1972: 13). The horrific dragon serpent ruler of the Ancient Ones (defeated by the Elder

Gods, the benevolent gods more closely associated with creation and humanity) is closely associated with Lovecraft and the Necronomicon's Cthulhu. 'It is this Tiamat or Leviathan that is identified closely with Cthulhu or Kutulu in the pages of the Necronomicon, although both names are mentioned independently of each other, indicating that somehow Kutulu is the male counterpart of Tiamat' (Simon 1977: xxi). Worshippers of Tiamat are associated with Kutulu, chaos, shape-shifting and unnatural alliances with beasts:

> [Know that the worshippers of Tiamat] are to be known by their seeming human appearance which has the mark of the beast upon them, as they change easily into the shapes of animals and haunt the Nights of Men ... and their books are the Books of Chaos and the flames, and are the Books of the Shadows and the Shells...and they are the raisers of the legions of maskim, the Liers-in-Wait. And they do not know what it is they do, but they do it at the demands of the serpent, at whose name even Ereshkigal gives fright and the dread Kutulu strains at his bonds. ('Book of Calling', Simon 1977: 97)

Feminine images of shells and shadows, of unpredictable potentiality, legion and chaos resonate around Tiamat, folded in the earth and the ocean. As an interesting parallel, the Magan Text and the Urilia Text of the *Necronomicon* warn against opening the gate of the abominations (over which Tiamat lords) because it is the abyss, the threshold between heaven and hell, earth and surface and life and death, Tiamat as cunt-gate-threshold, will open and 'all that abyss break forth upon the earth and the dead rise to eat the living for it is writ: And I will cause the dead to rise and eat the living' ('The Urilia Text', Simon 1977: 187). This parallel emphasizes the breakdown of the primary human bifurcation – life and death – when the divided is convoked not as polar but fold or threshold.

Although described as 'he', Kutulu (*The Necronomicon's* spelling of the more familiar Cthulhu) is a very cunty he. Kutulu is the many-tentacled squid-like creature that, like Leviathan/Tiamat, lies dead but dreaming in the depth of the ocean, where 'the water which is beneath the earth is feminine' (Enoch LIV.7–LV.2: 8, in Charles 2003). This is seen in Haraway's adaptation of tentacle theory in feminist entanglement ethics (in spite of Lovecraft also being embraced by speculative realists such as Graham Harman [2012] who seem to ask the other to oblige the observer, and by the existential angst of Michel Houellebecq [2008]). Hine's queering of Cthulhu resolves these either/or attributes by embracing the ecstasy of tentacular crepuscularity. Because Cthulhu's tentacles proliferate and emit from the aperture of his mouth, these tentacles could not be described as phallic. They primarily defy the unity of the phallus, and the phallus as penetrating, rather than originating, from the folds of flesh which constitute a corporeal aperture. We are also never told in Lovecraft or *The Necronomicon* what these tentacles do (like the disciples of Tiamat 'and they do not know what it is they do'). Their function, unlike the function of the phallus, is not laid down in advance, or indeed, at all. Cthulhu is an example of a masculine subject becoming-cunt. Humwawa, *The Necronomicon's* Lord of Abominations, has a face which is a mass of entrails. The face is the primary plane through which subjectivity is 'read' – gender, colour, race, sanity, class and sexuality. The gendered male white face represents the socially concealed phallus expressed in a visible and hence legible way. It is the zenith of the upright, frontal human, correlating the phallus with the head as seat of logic. The face is the head of the human form as itself entirely phallic. Humans do not have bodies. Anthropocentrism bestows faces and organized stratified corpuses emptied of visceral consistencies. The demonic ancient ones belong to the world of Antonin Artaud and Deleuze and Guattari's defacialized Bodies without Organs. Humwawa draws the cunt and the viscera to the most sacred plateau of the intelligible signified flesh; hence the becoming-cunt-face is its own form of becoming-cunt. The sigil or seal for Humwawa looks a lot like a cunt, while his brother Pazuzu is described as having rotting genitalia. Both abominations are male, yet both are explicitly described around their lack of phallocentric genitalia and unity in general. Rotting genitalia resonates with some of the less elegant descriptions of female genitalia as 'wound' or as a penis that has been castrated or gone wrong in some irredeemable way. Two of the key entities in *The Necronomicon* are female – Inanna and Hecate. In the Sumerian epic poem, Inanna travels to the underworld and is both mistress of heaven and hell, neither of which are repudiated. She is both shining spirit and rotting flesh, living and dead.

Why grigori do it better

The first part of Enoch is essentially about knowledge, creativity and thought and their relationship with desire as the ultimate punishable sin, concerning the Watchers, angels who fall because they mate with and teach knowledge to the women of earth. Inherently, the rethinking of the relationship between flesh, thought and desire becomes demonic and ruptures dominant 'Law'. The Watchers as angels are pure spirit. They fold spirit with the flesh of women, folding the imparting of knowledge with desire. The Watchers enflesh the threshold between man and God, or, to be precise, women and angels. This fold of woman and angel is an early example of invocation as a becoming. The unnatural participation between angel and woman is emphasized through angels being apparently sexless. How does one copulate to reproduce with a woman if one is not, technically, a man? Is birthing a monster, the cannibal Nephilim giants (whose gender is not referenced) that are the progeny of this union, reproduction or hybrid teratological production of singularities? Similarly, how can an angel be a demon at once? Is cacodaemonic copulation with a grigori cacodaemonic at all? Sexless or sexually ambiguous aligns with moral-less, or morally ambiguous. But the Watchers are only these things within a system of binaries that limit thought to two, one of two, and always isomorphic, where one of the two is clearly demarcated as better than the other. Where St John of the Cross uses esoteric Christianity to forsake and give up, St Theresa of Avila is an example of voluminous cacodaemonic copulation that produces proliferation without privation. If the Watchers are neither and more than both, just as the cunt is neither and more than the phallus, then convocation with Watchers is a neither and more than a sexual dialectic. A non-Euclidean act of desire? Itself a chaos ritual? Many texts written on the possibility of the Watchers being actual historical phenomena, aliens, angels. The Typhonian Order encourages such perspectives as encouraging a practitioner's most crucial ability as their capacity to interact with the nonhuman. The Watchers are bird-'men', or bird-human-angel entities, cross species and interkingdom, which, as we know, makes Leviticus very unhappy and probably puts them in the same food category as snakes, bats and pigs. Although 'eating' a Watcher could be a very interesting forbidden form of sexual ingestion. (I'll leave the 'no milk and meat together' law well alone here.) There is something less tangibly sinful in the union, sinful precisely because of its intangibility of forms, functions, desires and results. In her close reading of the Bible, biblical apocrypha and medieval angeology, Craddock blames human men for any sin perceived in the union between Watchers and women (2017: 20). God does not seem to punish the Watchers for their carnal transgression but for the imparting of knowledge, in a similar way to Eve being punished as a result, not of committing sin, but of receiving knowledge. (That she was seduced by a serpent resonates with the forms taken by Leviathan, Tiamat, Kutulu and other cunt-like deities.) The Watchers are punished by being relegated to the very cunt-like 'chasm of the abyss of the valley' (Enoch LV1: 3, in Charles 2003).

I have never decided whether the threshold entities of *The Necronomicon* and chaos magick using the Necronomicon as grimoire are the same Watchers as Enochian Watchers. Theirs is the middle symbol between human and demon-god in the necronomic sigil, and they must be evoked before a ritual. They do nothing, they are the active passive, the necessary present absent, the very entity of ambiguity, ambivalence and threshold. They occupy the gate and are the materiality of gate. 'Lovecraft's hero encounters strange animals, but he finally reaches the ultimate regions of a Continuum inhabited by unnameable waves and unfindable particles' (Deleuze and Guattari 1987: 248). Lovecraft describes worlds becoming-cunt, folding this dimension to reassemble all perception.

The very sun of heaven seemed distorted when viewed through the polarising miasma welling out from this sea-soaked perversion, and twisted menace and suspense lurked leeringly in those crazy elusive angles of carven rock where a second glance showed concavity after the first showed convexity. (1989: 94)

The self is inherently part of the folds and foldings in with these worlds until all perception is enveloped within a plane of Lovecraftian monsters and hybrids, from which the folded self cannot escape and often itself becomes infected with the contagion of the monstrous other plane. 'Then the other shapes began to appear, filling me with nameless horror the moment I awoke. But during the dreams they did not horrify me at all – I was one with them' (Lovecraft, 'The Shadow Over Innsmouth', 1994: 461). The terror of the altered familiar is also the wonder at the infinite possibilities of the already available not exchanged or repositioned but folded into a multidimensional band across which becoming cuts a trajectory forming unique consistency. This desire is accessed in chaos rituals, when they are performed not to access a result but a state. Large-scale demonstrations and direct actions can similarly operate along these lines. The activist corpus, made of molecular participants, accesses and disrupts the systems and institutes which only allow change on anthropocentric terms. Such disruption can alter the terms themselves and can be a tactic for various forms of mobile activism, without a unified centre or a leader.

A multiplicity is defined not by its elements, nor by a centre of unification or comprehension. It is defined by the number of dimensions it has; it is not divisible, it cannot lose or gain a dimension without changing its nature ... a multiplicity is continually transforming itself into a string of other multiplicities, according to its thresholds and doors. (Deleuze and Guattari 1987: 249)

The multiplicity of becoming-cunt as an assemblage reassembles the tensors and thresholds upon which it expresses force and by which force is expressed upon its various planes and dimensions. The self, the cunt and the world become threshold.

After loving monsters, Lovecraft's protagonists achieve a particle perception, a flattening out of all time and space where, instead of fold apprehension of perception being perspectival with each fold, perception becomes total and simultaneous. Cthulhu's 'nebulously recombining' (Lovecraft 1989: 99) eventually achieve 'eldritch contradictions of all matter, force and cosmic order' (Lovecraft 1989: 97). The base distortion of the horizon to no horizon apprehensible through any familiar perception reconfigures all angles of perception. Those who cannot cope go mad (in a more traditional sense), but those who allow themselves to dissipate into their dream worlds, scattering into particles. Bodies are more than fluid, becomings more than alliances. The self goes beyond being a point as limit as Leibniz claims, to becoming prolific points not mingled with other powers but simultaneous. Consciousness (external apprehension) and perception (internal apprehension) are, further, not simultaneous but non-differentiated, as they are from the consciousness of other particle-entities or forces. The Elder Gods are able to apprehend the infinite past and future in a vague immanence but this seems more presence as eternal than contraction – 'all that was and is and is to be exists simultaneously' (Lovecraft 1999a: 531). At the same time, memories are ablated and fears disappear. Peasley's dreams unfold in non-sequence sequence. Perception is defined as texture, entities as part matter, part indescribable as matter. Being 'wholly and horribly oriented' causes Peasley great trauma. The power to act, to enter into relation, the effectuation of folding through relations of celerity, force and affectuation is extended to a point of pure immanence, a trembling but not atrophy. Carter passes 'amidst backgrounds [both through and around] of other planets and systems and galaxies and cosmic continua; spores of eternal life drifting from world to world, universe to universe, yet all equally himself ... His self had been annihilated and yet he – if indeed there could, in view of that utter nullity of individual existence, be such a thing as he – was equally aware of being inconceivable way, a legion of selves' (Lovecraft 1999b: 526–7); The localism of the Carter-facet, Carter-fragment shows Lovecraft's protagonists move from becomings to molecular perception towards a state of pure existence-perception outside of linearity (time) – and aspectical apprehension (space) – a multiple and infinite unification, becoming-gods as the Elder Gods, the pure 'one'. In desperation Lovecraft attempts to describe Carter's infinity, terrestrial/non-terrestrial, living/dead, many-headed, many-tentacled, but he cannot describe it because it is neither perceivable nor conceivable. The best we can have is an encounter with the perception of the imperceptible.

The demon lover of magick ritual and lore creates a cuntly event. A shining darkness, an effulgent aberration who makes its partner a shining darkness, an effulgent aberration, 'a power of alliance inspiring illicit unions or abominable loves. This ... tends to prevent procreation; since the demon does not himself [sic] have the ability to procreate, he must adopt indirect means (e.g. the female succubus of a man and then becoming the male incubus of a woman, to whom he transmits the male semen)' (Deleuze and Guattari 1987: 246). Making a pact involves making a pack with the demon lover and abominates us. Pack/pacts are necessary for activism, with the unlike, with the unloved, the unknowable, the demonic. We become sorcerers, who invoke their lovers rather than being part of a structure which limits their selections. 'The sorcerer has a relation of alliance with the demon as the power of the anomalous' (Deleuze and Guattari, 1987: 246). The cunt is the first and most powerful anomaly in human anatomy, physiology and, thus, the taxonomy of life. Rituals of daemonic convocation involves the gifting of self to other and accepting the other of self that may be encountered but not revealed. It gives the other of self, or the outside, to self and gives self to the risk and chance of the outside-of-self. Cuntly chaosium desire folds outside in on self and hence the self becomes crevice into which the outside slips or sacrificial wound into which the other bleeds. The outside-of-self is then gifted to the outside as our awareness (but not knowledge) of it is invoked by the outside. Cunt chaos accepts the death of self in the plethora of desire, sacrificing the self to the chance which magick desire necessitates.

If neither the invisibility in the visible, nor the unthought in desire can be known, the outside of self expresses the unself or unsubject of self. Experiencing a chaos union raises the impossibility of self in the face of the force without, there is no other positioned in opposition to self, but the subject no less dissipates, into what Guattari calls degree zero point of implosion. Dissipation is ecstasy, violence in the sacrifice of self, inner violence in the face of unshakeable consent that makes us tremble. The cunt-I is a trembling, chaos desire a redistribution of trembling, becoming-cunt the unbearable pain within the pleasure of desire and the incandescent daemon a lover we take, a spirit we invoke, an entity with which we fold, and to which we consent, giving the gift of self we cannot give, to die in the ecstasy of the outside-of-self, outside of perception, outside of time, outside of this world, but no less materially within experience and reality.

5

Embracing death

Natural affirmation: Sketches for the end of the Anthropocene

'*Will and understanding are one and the same*' (Spinoza 1957: 200). Death and affirmation are seemingly contradictory terms. Death is usually posited in opposition with life, and affirmation with negation, so affirmation resonates with life and death with negation. In this structure, death is the negation of a life, presuming a being which is absent. Life is the affirmation of presence, or life is affirmed by the acknowledgement of a presence. The interrelationship between these four terms – death, life, negation and affirmation – emerges simultaneously through their orientation around a being or the 'being' of a being. Death is of something that already is and ceases to be, thus negating a being; life affirms the being of a being already in existence. Negating a living being brings death to that being, its rights or freedom; affirming a being's life also affirms its rights and freedom. From a humanist perspective, the problem of being precedes life and death, affirmation and negation, rights and freedom. From a natural or ecosophical perspective, life and death, affirmation and negation either precede or erupt with being, and being is neither problem nor given, but becomes increasingly a detrimental concept. Detrimental for whom? Challenging the being of a being is clearly detrimental for that being, yet this challenge has formed the foundation of metaphysical query and the capacity to challenge one's own being usually comes after the luxury of being counted as a being, so the detriment is similarly luxurious. It certainly has little or no relation to death, and by abstracting the force of existing, it also becomes only tentatively related to life. The problem for the ahuman ecosophist is that counting as a being is a luxury afforded to few, and it is a practice of recognition which dismembers the world into a hierarchical series of over-emphasized fragments atop useful secondary not-beings who may or may not be dividuated from each other, and a general murky soup of 'everything else'. As Seyla Benhabib sees the death of man as one of the three tenets of post-structural ethics, along with the death of history and the death of truth (1992), this chapter will suggest that in the age of the anthropocene, the death of the human is a necessity for all life to flourish and relations to become ethical. Death in this sense has been integral to much post-structural philosophy. If we understand death as a finitude of certain patterns of knowledge or compulsions in existence, a simultaneous unravelling deconstruction which leads to something creative and new rather than cessation, then we have in brief the death of being towards becomings for Deleuze and Guattari, the death of power producing critical relations of force in Foucault, the death of the symbolic and human language giving way to semiotic experimentation in Kristeva, the death of the subject/object divide producing mucosal love in Irigaray, the death of the social order driven by the parasitic human in favour of a natural contract in Serres, the death of capitalist institutionalized consciousness opening the machinic unconscious in Guattari and so on. Death of the human subject in its Vitruvian manifestation is inherent in each of these philosophies. This chapter will take its cue from these life-affirming deaths but posit actual death as part of these philosophical affirmations, where the death of the other and of living connections must be accounted for as an unethical diminishing of allowing the other their expressive force, and the death of the human body in its actual existence more than just as a pattern of subjective agency is a real option for an ahuman ecosophical ethics.

Motive

What has this discussion of death and life, the natural world and human systems got to do with affirmation? Just as will and ethics collapse all binaries, I wish to collapse the binaries of natural life and death insofar as they are usually correlated with affirmation and negation by proposing that the death of the human species is the most life-affirming event that could liberate the natural world from oppression, and our death could be an act of affirmative ethics which would far exceed any localized acts of compassion because those acts will be bound by human contracts, social laws and the prevalent status of beings, things and their placement within knowledge.

When death remains within potestas and is therefore aligned within an isomorphic binary hierarchy which would oppose it to life and group it with negation, it raises spectres of apathy and despair. The problem with death is as much the problem with the system in which it emerges, the same anthropocentric system whereby the human emerges limited to a certain form of signified subject, not necessarily a life. In reference to the four terms I wish to allow to interact – life, death, affirmation and negation – I will use two examples to elucidate the problems, thinking through them within the anthropocentric system pose and thus why the anthropocene is resistant to these problems. Within a natural contract, ecosophical relations neither oppose the four terms nor vilify the examples I will offer. There are many, many examples which can be chosen. The history of resistance is paved with similar activist actionable examples, and all social movements which resulted in changes towards minoritarian humans can be cited. Feminism, anti-racism, disability rights, queer theory, LGBTQI rights and others grappled with the anthropocentric system. Equality seeks to raise the less-than-human to the level of the pinnacle of the anthropocene's pyramid, difference to eradicate the pyramid itself, so equality works with potestas and difference with potentia, equality with homogeneity and difference with alterity. Equality is contingent on its relation with use and value, difference with recognition and metamorphosis, so even these terms are not clear. Each has their benefits for real lived liberation of minoritarians. All these movements remain grappling with the 'problems' they seek to resolve in opening new modes of relations, and, crucially, all are activist philosophies with material histories of events and affects that have benefitted lived experiences. All as well are affirmative activisms as they seek to create and open the world rather than limit or destroy anything beyond oppressive power. Where I wish to push things is through the incorporation of the death of the human species in actuality and to cease the actual death of the nonhuman other as inherently joyful affirmative qualities of protest, and this I see exemplified in two activist philosophies which result in two material actions: human extinction and animal abolition. These two areas have varying degrees of difference in their current manifestations, but neither has received extensive philosophical address in the way gender, race and other human activisms have as affirmative and joyful. Both are still considered relatively extreme and even belonging to the realm of grass-roots extreme activism (or, in the case of animal abolitionists, even terrorism), which separates them from the world of 'serious' theory or philosophy. So my ideas may seem sketched rather than exhaustive. But their place in alterity studies has never been more urgent than life in the throes of the annihilative grasp of the anthropocene, and the quality they share is death, that the death of the human affirms all life.

Human extinction is still a sparse, loose idea advocated by sometimes opposing groups. Most obviously, there is the Voluntary Human Extinction Movement (VHEMT), the Church of Euthanasia and efilism, the latter of which will be addressed separately. VHEMT is somewhat divided between those who wish the human race to cease population in order to eradicate human overpopulation and its exhaustion and destruction of the earth, and those who also choose not to breed but see an apocalyptic horizon and operate under an 'every man for himself' attitude of immanent hedonism 'for tomorrow we die'. Ahumanism subscribes to no singular human extinction group, but clearly the message of the former sector of the group is more in keeping with the affirmative benefits of human death. The Church of Euthanasia has as its four stations of the cross sodomy, suicide, abortion and cannibalism. In their activism towards the end of human life on the planet, their posthumanism interestingly resonates with human minoritarian activism. Roughly, these correlate as sodomy with queer (where sodomy is defined as any non-reproductive sexual act, including masturbation, asexuality and heterosexual intercourse with no intention of procreation), abortion with female/feminist sexuate rights, cannibalism with animal rights, where human carcasses are used as a source of food instead of murdering animals, and suicide with agency over one's own life and thus death, including euthanasia with disability rights in reference to the right to die versus the enforcement of life on those who express a wish to die but cannot execute their own death. It shouldn't need to be pointed out that neither group advocates murder or eugenics (however ironically that may sit considering the murder advocated by sanctioned capital and war machines). These are two of the longest established of now many groups advocating human extinction, and as stated above, ahumanism aligns with none in particular. I chose these two to show that human extinction can be lamentative but also affirmative and does tend to align with an ecosophical and minoritarian philosophy rather than any violent, genocidal war machine mentality one may expect from the utterance 'human extinction'. At the most simple level, this chapter sees the decision not to reproduce and the right to suicide under any circumstances as viable and necessary forms of activism and the extension of life through biotechnology at any cost as a symptom of multinational industry, where life extension means profit rather than a simply altruistic practice. Put very simply, human extinction can be understood as a good idea for ecosophical ethics and need not be considered 'unthinkable' but can be welcomed as affirmative of earth life. The second example I will use continues the central ethic of the manifesto by emphasizing the ahuman practice of animal abolitionism. Abolitionism seeks no reason for the other to defend itself and thus vindicate its right to expression based on its equivalence with the human. It seeks to abolish all interaction with animals based on a human superiority presumption, and its activist forms involve ending vivisection, boycotting and protesting circuses, sea parks and zoos, and practicing veganism in order to stop the murder of trillions of animals annually, while, like all activist groups, including human extinction and feminism, there is much internal splintering based on varying opinions as to 'how' and 'why' the centre of abolition of use remains consistent. While human extinction welcomes the actual death of the human due to its measurable benefit on ecosophical interactions (or, perhaps more correctly, due to the measurable detriment humans have on the planet and even the solar system), abolition refuses the actual torture and death of the other and especially the use of the superiority of the human in 'nature' to vindicate the acts, because the rhetoric of vindication abstracts actual pain and death and converts the real physicality of the nonhuman other into an idea between humans, thus refusing to acknowledge its unethical affect of relations. These two ahumanisms coalesce human death as affirmation in a number of ways, which I will explore below, beginning with why it is difficult to see affirmation in these two activisms while we remain within the anthropocentric structure of action.

Choosing the death of humankind remains possibly the most unthinkable thing for the anthropocene; however, in terms of a universality which traverses domains, worlds and heterogeneous voices, placing the referential self outside of power and knowledge towards new virtual universes, with their unpredictable and unknowable affects, emphasizes that universality is of *all* life and its irreducible connectivity. Currently we see the rise of the 'Extinction Rebellion' deploying direct action, a tactic also utilized by abolitionist groups and euthanasia groups. The extinction rebellion remains anthropocentric at heart, because it sees the threat of ecological crisis primarily through the lens of a threat to human survival. It makes no room for the grace of stepping aside and embracing human extinction so that the world may flourish, which would be the most effective form of rebellion against individual death, the death of diversity or species extinction (which is an inherently speciesist impulse anyway when the perpetuation of species in breeding programmes at zoos is tantamount to slavery so human offspring do not miss out on the spectacle of another species member). Reproducing humans reproduces the anthropocene as a system. The very default nature of the expectation to breed, even before the gender-oppressive and the heteronormative elements are considered, shows no self-reference and thus no activism. While cries of 'My child won't be bad' or 'I will raise my child differently' inevitably arise, such claims presume the family unit is extricable from society. *All life* is subsumed by the anthropocene, so any human life is ripe for reproducing its ideology. The decision not to breed is seen as treacherous to one's species by its extreme critics, but ethically the expressions of and affects from another human on the world far outweigh any benefits, and all the various scenarios which posit one special child rely on the futurity Spinoza states are unethical and superstitious. Affirmation here comes from the necessity of connecting to other heterogeneous voices and pathways when the reproduction of the same species is forsaken, rather than being childless, being an 'absence' of something that never existed anyway. Ironically, perhaps, there is a great divide in abolitionist activism between vegan breeders and anti-breeders due to some vegans, like most breeders, being convinced that their child will be formed perfectly in their own or a better image.

But similarly and against traditional humanist and even modernist claims, the post-enlightenment eternal quest to know the self as the prime empirical transcendental metaphysical phenomenon also negates, through nomenclature and exhaustion, the very life it seeks to know, and is a deathbound necrophilosophy. Human reproduction is a notorious reason many cite to overcome their fear they are not immortal. But of course the self does not live on in the child; the investment of immortality in a future non-existent life repudiates the here-and-now lives, human and nonhuman, with which creative beneficial ethical encounters can be established.

Potentia and its affirmations

The way negation and affirmation have been aligned with certain phenomena are arbitrary. They can be traced as much from a religious understanding of privation which overvalues the self by denying it as from a Heideggerian Daesin-centric world view where to deny self would be to deny the world and embrace death. But each age has its negations and affirmations which correlate with certain practices. Within the anthropocene, and especially considering its intimacy with consumption, the 'right' to exploit animals and the 'right' to reproduce ignite fiery arguments where the exorcized spectre of 'need' over want is invoked, and crucially for my argument, both abolitionist practices and the decision not to breed are defaulted to a form of negation of those rights rather than their place as activist-affirmative practices.

Not breeding is not negation: Without wishing to engage the world of absence/presence and other post-structural grapples with existence, the presumed position of most is that humans must reproduce. The species argument is balanced by fear of eugenics – yes there are too many humans to sustain the planet, but the moment we need to decide who reproduces and who doesn't, we enter dubious moral territory. Rarely is the definitive need of the species at all engaged. Following Spinoza, ethical interactions are immanent, and the imposing future ignores the affective potentials of inevitable and sought interactions. Against Spinoza, I value nonhuman life equally to human, and I do not see human life as always striving to live, especially in terms of the desire for euthanasia, suicide or the 'lives-to-come' of unborn generations. Irrefutably, there are a *lot* of humans on the earth. The tendency to privilege species, which has also refined to privilege certain humans over others, occurs concentrically in the tendency to privilege bloodlines and kinship over other human-to-human species interaction, and is equally as arbitrarily and offensively prejudiced. Activism towards human extinction does not necessarily mean loathing of one's own species, just the detrimental effects of its continuation. Covertly loving humans and children rarely translate into loving all but more often loving *mine*, either had or yet to be. Thinking immanent lives with the lives that are here and now creates communities without kinship and 'it is now a question of knowing whether relations (and which ones?) can compound directly to form a new, more "extensive", relation or whether capacities or whether capacities can compound more directly to constitute ... How can a being take another being into its world, but while preserving and respecting the other's own relations and world' (Deleuze 1988: 126). Breeding and valuing kinship and bloodlines negates the other. Human extinction affirms interaction with those lives here and emphasizes their matter (and that they matter) while preserving the earth and the natural world from the parasitic actions of a continuing human species. As an added bonus, it would also repudiate any gender-essentialist argument due to there being no real need for sexually dimorphic discrimination. Human extinction, in its certain unique slowness and speed, would formulate an entirely new mode of necessary interaction that would rely on creativity and novelty, and would affirm the potentialities of the human mind to formulate these creative practices.

Life, need and death

It is the ultimate postmodern irony that in the age of the anthropocene, resources that are made of the antediluvian dead flesh of ancient creatures through oils and fossil fuels are fast running out, and we manufacture and convert to consumable objects the lives of nonhuman animals, yet the human body, whether alive or dead, especially when it appears in its Vitruvian manifestation, remains a sacred spectacle of the absence of presence consolidated into a cadaver mausoleum. This chapter celebrates a reversal of status and values the cadaver as both a material resource and repressed symbol of death activism, through its potentials as food, as lover, as an untapped fuel which offers possibilities that pervert both the dominance of the human and the need to queer our relationship with death and corpses.

To suggest that death is a vitalistic aspiration acknowledges the paradox that comes from demarcating one's individual life from the world. As a living entity, the anthropocentric is essentially parasitic. The majority of humans who are not what Serres calls 'semiconductors' (2007: 5) – that is, they take monodirectionally and never give – ironically are often forced into a non-wilful parasitism where their taking is a mode of survival that can convert need to greed, albeit in our accursed anthropocentric shares we are far beyond the psychoanalytic differentiation between need and want even while we watch others die of needing while wanting. Philosophers of vitalism suggest that vitalism only refers to need as it relates to life, which conjoin in antipathy to death as the negative force that gives life its vigour, so to speak. Frederic Worms conjoins need between the minimum need and extensive need, sustenance and duration, while grappling with how vitalism can define itself vitalistically without simply being reduced to the avoidance of death (2015: 47–8). Miguel De Beistegui suggests that any measure of life, be it through survival need or extensivity, is reduced to economic measure and antagonistic to the presence of either pleasure or desire, namely *jouissance* (2015: 256). The current philosophical fascination with how we can define life seems admirable in its reactivity to the deathbound world where disinterest and fatalism occurs collaterally due to exponential growth of money and privileged human life as our perceived measure of anthropocentric success. This defaults death to a somehow unenviable state which is arbitrary. For some, perhaps not many even, death's promise is jouissance. In certain cases such as terminal suffering, this would seem apparent, but there is a considerable argument for allowing people to actively and activistly take the death they desire without seeing the maintenance of human life as a priori the primary goal of existence. To those who struggle to survive, the embrace of a desire for death may seem luxuriant, but this template cannot hold true for those with the capacity for a desire for death. While we conveniently lay our lazy arguments on the idea that to want to die simply because life does not hold the same pleasure for all individuals is a Western fantasy driven by excess and ennui, we ignore the suffering and mass murder of all kinds of nonhumans and humans around the world that sustain the existence the West and emergent economies see as their right but that is nothing more than gluttonous parasitism. To be truly reciprocal, the parasite must give death in place of the death it inherently takes. This matter is complicated further by the rising examples of the lack of grace or mercy when the individual is denied death in an equivalent way to the oppressed denied a bearable life. Bifo invokes the example of the prevention of suicide at factories in Korea, and the refusal of Chinese factories to give suicided workers' families payouts, reflecting the long practice of Western insurance refusing to acknowledge that semiocapitalism has meant the choice between fiscal relief for one's family or continued life at the expense of a quality living. To these and many other examples, Bifo points out that capitalism's 'response is to create new zombies, through the spectre of death without compensation' (2015: 181). On the one hand, we are denied suicide and for the accursed it is the luxury need we cannot afford; on the other, we cannot comprehend the willingness of the self to die for something greater seen in certain terrorist acts. While these acts are deplorable in their aggression, it is the unimaginability of self-induced death that most media coverage sees as so indignancy-inducing. And yet even as posthumans we are faced with the most tiring of questions, especially perpetuated by transhumanism but essentially present everywhere, which is, Why should we want to live? Diachronous thought always places death on the side of despair and nihilism, where to not answer the 'why' means to not bother. Ahumanism sees whining about the unfairness of the meaninglessness of life and the inevitability of death in nihilism, or the disobedience to God/State/Work in despair, as tedious luxuries that ultimately only show an enslavement to either a greater master of anthropocentric making, be it an institute or one's own ego. I do not make demands on anyone to prove their life is worth living, but neither do I see someone coveting an exit from life, which would reduce resource consumption and, in many cases, their own disdain for life, as to be absolutely avoided at all costs. What interests me is not questions of circumstance or new legislation for euthanasia but the troubling idea that what we are denied most rigorously the more we are perceived to have succeeded is our own death, and, thus, by implication, our life is not our own. Meanwhile, death of the human by denial of resources happens across all societies, but if that human is not recognized as valuable, it is simply seen as some bizarre vindication of a socioeconomic distorted 'Darwinianism', especially at this time in the UK where the disabled and poor are dying while the rich see success in their capital value, pretending it is not inherited.

The continuation of diachrony in perceptions of life and death spreads across a form of antinatalism essentially co-opted from a kind of Western fetishism of Buddhism, namely efilism. Coming etymologically from the reverse of 'life', efilism claims it is better to have never been. Efilist philosophers such as David Benatar hinge their arguments on basic binaries of pleasure and pain which roughly correlate to good and bad and extend to a vindication of life and death. Efilism has a vague correspondence with utilitarianism but emphasizes the suffering of life over utilitarianism's greater good. Both are absolute in their perception of the capacity to evaluate which is which, making both dependent on economic measure of value as an either/or, and to an extent both rely on (anthropocentric) determinism. Efilism's redeeming feature is that it promotes antinatalism, and often veganism, in its aspirations to a reduction in suffering, and this attitude promises potentials for opening the world through the cessation of the human. However, efilism's claim that all life, human and nonhuman, should be ceased is a hubris I am not convinced humans have the right to exert. While the cessation of suffering humans cause is already manipulated in a way that could come under an efilist rubric, these 'management' tools usually come in the form of culling populations of nonhumans to redress an imagined environmental balance most usually caused by humans in the first place. Domestic efilism such as neutering rescue animals is necessary, especially when rescuing can involve the speciesism of feeding one slaughtered animal to sustain another, and neutering humans is the logical way to prevent the perpetuation of this practice as well. Ahumanism has no signifying lens so all humans should be neutered; this is the polar opposite of eugenics. Perhaps it is better to see it as more of an inoculation of the earth against the virus of humans. And those who have never been cannot suffer, so there is nothing materially wrong with neutering all humans. What is disappointing about efilism is the adherence to an either/or evaluation of experience and life that sometimes reeks of a lamentation of existential crisis. This may explain why so many efilists are the stereotypical white male angst pessimists who seek to enhance the reputation of pessimism. There are rising activisms from a more traditionally feminist and queer perspective, such as the Queer Death Studies Network (QDSN) that originated in Sweden, which manifests:

> QDSN serves as a site for 'queering' traditional ways of approaching death both as a subject of study and philosophical reflection, and as a phenomenon to articulate in artistic work or practices of mourning. Here, the notion of 'queer' conveys many meanings. It refers to researching and narrating death, dying and mourning in the context of queer bonds and communities, where the subjects involved/studied/interviewed and the relations they are involved in are recognized as 'queer'. Simultaneously, the term 'queer' can also function as an adverb and a verb, referring thus to the processes of going beyond and unsettling (subverting, exceeding) binaries and given norms, normativities, and constraining conventions. In other words, 'queer' becomes both a process and a methodology that is applicable and exceeds the focus on gender and sexuality as its exclusive concerns.

QDSN sees the vitalism and the assemblage configuration of ecosophical and disciplinary relations as part of a world where the tentative subject is expansive, acting as a foil to the sometimes godlike perspective of the efilist who draws the world into their own singular ego. While the QDSN does not necessarily advocate veganism and antinatalism, my experience as a member has shown these are underlying foundational principles where such activism is celebrated without being perceived as privation, and with a sense of care in practices even while embracing the finitude of life. This opposes some aspects of certain VHEMT ideologies that in the embrace of finitude can often lead to hedonistic practices which are more akin to the idea that because we will all be dead soon we should take what we wish and do what we please, a sort of efilism where the pain is inevitable so should be distributed at will. As a celebration of queer death activism and an alternative to the finitude that verges on despair of some efilist and VHEMT ideas, I will now shift register to suggest more ecstatic modes of queer death activism, an activism neither of privation nor loss but jubilance, even eroticism.

Queering the dead

The following section will utilize queering the dead to manifest a joyous way of love that may see death become both practical and also an expression of creative activism. I am in love with death. Death seems the most natural and desirable attractive manifestation of a concept and an encounter (un)imaginable. Its trajectories of desire – cannibalism, necrophilia, delirium, mysticism and ecstasy – compose a world of wonder which opens limitless imagination in the face of a vibrant, teeming nothingness both inconvertible to language and unthinkable to knowledge. That death-sex is transgressive is both a redundancy and a true comment on what this world really fears, which is atrophied in its own unique sort of death, but of a different order. I love death as the encounter between nature – the before and inevitable of flesh – and the ahuman – the beyond constraining systems of capital, signification and normativity (this beyond is found in the arts and wherever we wish to 'escape' the vile position of the dominating human). In between nature and the ahuman is the social contract. This is the mesh of intersecting economic, moral, legislative and medicalizing orders which define, militarize and pattern life on earth, dominated by and for (a particular kind of) human. This contract fears death, it repudiates death; however, for creativity and for a life lived in flesh, it is entirely dead. Its eternal repetition of hierarchies which utilize endlessly adaptable but ultimately empty circulating signifiers reducible to nothing more than capital exchange commodities and popularity currency denies us both our flesh and lives found not in labour, consumption and surplus but in *living* – living immanently, living as a nowness and a quality singular and unrepeatable. Why is the social contract – immobile, catatonic, atrophied and to all appearances as dead as a thing can be – so afraid of actual death and the delights it may bring? Because the collision of sex and death requires a visceral signified for the sign (that being the actual flesh, the *real* flesh) without a moral or legislative structure that both brings it into being for society and simultaneously effaces its fleshy specificity in time and space. The social contract converts all things to codes of exchange in a system of value, so in a way, it has neither death nor life. Death as an irrefutable natural and inevitable phenomenon is denied. It is replaced by statistics, by laws, by headlines. But actual death belongs to the judges, the medical examiners, not to the people and their own lives. In death we find not simply the transgression of taboo but also the transgression of free ownership of our lives and the delights to be found in the former flesh of others as a queer celebration beyond identity, beyond gender, beyond sexuality, even beyond politics, certainly when the most useless object, the corpse, becomes useful, even desirable, we have spat in the eye of a social contract that both denies and conceals the very existence of the corpse. So here we have it – the life of the corpse as an object of desire, and the ways in which acknowledging death as natural vilifies the hypocrisy and emptiness of the social contract that keeps us in its perpetual living death.

Deleuze states, 'Anthropomorphism … should be corrected by the Nietzschean principle that there is a subjectivity to the universe which is no longer anthropomorphic but cosmic' (2006: 41). Speaking of active and reactive forces and eternal return, we could say that living the life of a subjectified signified human is a being in denial of their becoming (which is always already death) and maintaining that structure is a reactive force, while welcoming death is an active force to the extent it would require imagination. This could explain both our fascination with death, zombies, vampires and abstracted dead who are also ahuman becomings. Cannibalism and necrophilia are *interesting*. While we manifest our automaton little lives and repudiate death, the more vain of us imagine our death to be a great and spectacular or at least interesting event, and if we are very lucky, an event that is both libidinal and visceral, eros and thanatos. Death is banal, everyday, inevitable and elaborate, creative, thoughtful; it denies reactive and repetitive narratives; it refuses being victim based on traditional oppressive regimes. It is the final queer act. And one more thing (and I speak here again as an extinctionist). Being nothing and being inconsequential based on how we are defined is freedom, not death of the subject. Being a body involves losing the subjectivity of the self. It is alimentary, erotic and death of self. It does not invoke or involve the depressing nihilism of efilism or some Apollonic speculative realism and object oriented ontology. It is an absolute Dionysian celebration.

A proviso: the celebration of the corpse and of death here is entirely mutual and consensual. The business (for that is what it is) of murder and death machines from the farm to the battlefield is the realm of the social contract. Even the murderer belongs to headlines and psychiatry. I wish to celebrate the banal reality that everyone dies but not in order to vindicate enforcing death, which belongs to the death machines of the right wing, of war, of dematerializing death in the name of an ideology or an abstract ideal that conceals a will to power, simply the material inevitability that resists the kinds of reich thinking that removes living organisms from their existence; the potential of the already corpse for desire (found in necrophilia, cannibalism and other thanaterotics); the life of oneself that may bring more joy through its cessation (from euthanasia to auto-thanaterotics to suicide without pathologization of the psyche). This then can convert to the political realm where the radical limit of queer politics can offer human extinction as a freedom from repetition and the decimation of the earth and ecology to the death of identity and thus identity politics which means we can create collectives based on the unlike, community based on alterity and difference. Production of alliances without reproduction. Queer families of unlikes but not kin without mutual consent. Nations of global assemblages without ownership of anything, especially the bodies and territories of others. Absolute ownership of our own bodies and what we can become as a host through them upon death. I want to create an ahuman thanaterotics based on love, not aggression. Death and the utilization of the corpse seems founded by default on a very precise cultural and historical trajectory of the connection between violence and being in proximity with the dead. This occurs by two means. The first is that the dead body is not divested of its personhood, even while the body of a nonhuman animal is never bestowed agency, simply murdered to be cannibalized. The second is that tales of necrophilia and cannibalism are designed to titillate via celebrations of misogyny and imperialist racism. Sometimes even together. Many animal rights critics, especially Adams and myself, have pointed out the intended denigrative misogyny and racism of language utilizing the bestial metaphor uniting nonhuman animals, women and people of colour. Good, I say. I welcome it more than being denounced as a social contractor. Similarly, the fascination for the serial killer or domestic abuser (almost always white men) who either kills to have sexual relations with a corpse or to eat another human is denounced as both savage and primitive. This default relation between violence and the utilisation of the corpse is arbitrary and driven by a fear of death conjoined with a hatred of the victim, usually but not always women, sometimes of the killers own self as an internalized version of homophobia, overcome with acts of necrophilia and cannibalism. Freud here is anything but old-fashioned. He queries what happens to civilization if communism wins, if property ownership is dissolved, because he sees the demarcation of objects and primarily their meaning for the individual as the trigger (I use that term in its most contemporary sense as well as the *fort-da*) for the inherent aggression in man (sic but also not sic in this instance). 'The instinct of destruction', he writes, 'moderated and tamed, and as it were, inhibited in its aim, must when it is directed toward objects, provide the ego with satisfaction of its vital needs and with control

over nature' (Freud 1961: 81). The two key components of the death
drive that convert to aggression here are ego and control. Freud's
language sees civilization in the same way as we could suggest
Serres does. Controlled, an exertion of power in the maintenance
of the anthropocentric ego. Both elements take the world as objects
designed for and at the mercy of the parasitic human subject. This
is the configuration by which the connection between violence and
necrophilia and cannibalism has emerged, and the structure of that
configuration is no different to the structure that facilitates and
normalizes malzoan practices, environmental rape, displacement of
indigenous peoples and native species. This pop form of serial-killer
necro cannibalism is a microcosm of normative anthropocentric
practice. I propose a different understanding of these practices.
Either way, the corpse remains.

In the thanaterotics of love, the corpse occurs without
anthropocentric violence as a necessary given, especially a dialectic
of subject/object violence. I do not wish to entirely extricate the
possibility of corpse erotics if the corpse comes from mass violence
perpetrated by governments, wars or pollutants, but my point is that
the corpse has occurred or arrived. The human is not hunted, the
corpse is not created against its own agency, but should the person
desire becoming-corpse this should be facilitated. The corpse exists
for us only after its status as corpse. Currently the corpse retains more
rights than living organisms and nonhuman animals. The law and
judiciary enunciation define the status of the organism more than
gross perceptible agency. Humans are statistics both alive and dead,
but always just statistics. Cannibalism of humans by humans is not
against nature; it is against the law. It is against white, male Western

phallocentric understandings of respect for the dead, which is nothing more than a masquerade of a denial of death for a variety of reasons. What does the ahuman say to the law, if the motive is love and the act does not deny the other agency? It says, 'Eat the anthropocene'. The law, which divides the world into ownerships, which divides humans into subjects, which creates a hierarchy over bare life and repudiates nature and earth, holds no dominion over nature's ethical ecosophy. The law murders, the law plunders. Nature does not. Bellegarrigue's 1850 *Anarchist's Manifesto* (2002) primarily critiques power and ownership as the source of misery, the two elements Freud demarcated as the creators of aggression. Punk transformed Bellegarrigue's message into a clearer and quite appealing one: 'Eat the rich'. Andrade responds similarly to the imposition of the social contract by imperialism in his 1928 *Cannibal Manifesto*: 'I asked a man what was Right. He answered me that it was the assurance of the full exercise of possibilities. That man was called Galli Mathias. I ate him' (1991: 46). The law says cannibalism is evil but plunder and murder are good for civilization. Nietzsche's maxim 153 is, 'That which is done out of love always takes place beyond good and evil' (1973: 103). Environmental historian Ellen Stroud emphasizes that in dealing with corpses, the moral cues of the social contract are often outraged before or beyond what the law can imagine in reference to what people do with their beloved dead. She states,

> When you read something upsetting like that [a woman charged with concealing a death, after it was discovered she had kept her mother's corpse in her home], it's easy to assume that it must be against the law. But when it comes to dead bodies, laws often don't

exist until someone transgresses a norm. People might not even realize that there is a norm until someone crosses what they see as a line ... I find it interesting that people aren't outraged or even surprized to hear about a neighbor burying a German shepherd in the backyard, even though a German shepherd can practically be as big as a person. But a person in the front yard: That's not OK. (Woolsten 2018)

Cannibalism has various offensive and stupid trajectories – postcolonial anthropological fetish ending in blaming indigenous populations for contracting Creutzfeldt-Jakob disease due to their 'primitive' cannibalistic ways, to the assumption (seen in many representations) that cannibalism need be a result only of a violent death, very similar to many documentations and representations of cannibalism's bedfellow necrophilia. Cannibalism is necessarily none and independent of these. Our world is groaning under the weight of the parasitic pestilence of human life and yet our excessive resource is the human dead. We breed, torture, torment and murder entire enslaved species for moments of epicurean familiarity that essentially converts the vital, independent and rich life of the other into our own faecal matter. And yet we have a perverse relationship with rituals of human death to preserve the idea that human life persists in the devotional relic of the corpse. I say, if you must eat meat, you can without being malzoan. Eat the dead human.

Cannibalism is queer in its collapse of subject and object and food and sex. No surprise in the world of consumerism that collapses everything to purchase. Except cannibalism could be a phenomenally cheap, if not free, resource. It involves what we would hitherto define as an unnatural relation with unworthy trash, but aren't all us queers already far beyond that? 'These combinations are neither genetic nor structural; they are interkingdoms, unnatural participations. That is the only way Nature operates – against itself' (Deleuze and Guattari 1987: 242). And while the avoidance of Creutzfeldt-Jakob disease seems a tiny blip on the road to anthropophageous resource abundance, the moral question is absolutely redundant: 'Nature has no particular goal in view, and final causes are mere human figments' (Spinoza 1957: 174–5). Death is natural. The leftover corpse is natural. Even if we are not malzoans, the corpse could go to the maintenance of enslaved species unable to be liberated, such as rescue nonhuman animals, or to fuel. The murder of the other to eat when it is unnecessary seems entirely unnatural, a social contract, a jurisprudence of anthropocentric hubris of the most unpalatable and vulgar kind. Cannibalism is ethically elegant in comparison. A gift from death. The human parasite become host. Our resistance to hosting even in death exacerbates our already deplorable environmental practices. Cannibalism is cosmic ethics. All we are is humans. All we have the right to destroy, to negotiate, to enslave, is ourselves, and we seem adept at doing it to each other, but it's time to say enough to imposing this potestas on to other species in favour of utilizing our own limitless potentia. It's time for organ donation to become food donation.

The body

The body dies. Humanism, transcendentalism, religion all pretend it won't happen. Then after it happens, they pretend it doesn't exist, or it enters into a metempsychosis of eternal transformation, or its disposal is hyper-ritualized to protect our understanding that it didn't really happen. Yet human corpses in art, film, literature and all creative spaces where desire expresses creativity have afforded limitless unravellings of the flesh. Not necessarily aggressive or violent, the act of exploration of the post-human flesh is an act of love. Just as Guattari and Artaud claim that human-signifying systems massacre the body by naming and thus limiting every part, every function and every potential, and they urge us to become bodies without organs, that is, without organization imposed by organisations, so the dead body is the limitless lover that collapses all memory, identity, organization and appropriate use. Necrophilia, cannibalism, memorializing fetishism, surgical intrigue, the potentials of the dead body for desire and as a resource are without end and far exceed the pathologizing names psychology and anthropology have given them and the law allows. Where is the transgression in creatively desiring and exploring the dead human body? We murder nonhumans in terrifying numbers, we annihilate those humans unlike us through exploitation. Transgressing the corpse taboo encourages an exploration of the corporeality of the repressed flesh of the subject and demands a visceral imagination beyond bifurcations of sex and death, desire and disgust, the erotic and the alimentary, identity and materiality. Go forth and love the dead!

Life

Our faith in freedom is as deluded as any other faith. One issue which affirms this adamantly is our estrangement from our own lives. We neurotically immerse ourselves in identity politics and in the identities of others, overcoding our simple fleshly living with strata of subjectification from the homogenizing mass collective to the minutely individual, but still we are compelled to speak ourselves as what we are. Not *that* we are. And certainly not that we may not want to be. The ultra-stylized identity politics of issues has merged with the consumerism of capital seduction so that our lives, bodies and identities are a series of lists of symbolic demarcations that create walls, barriers, meaningless 'communities'. The living of life disappears. For those who struggle to live we don't want to know, because we cannot recognize their dearth of symbols and their distance to the reality of flesh is too intimate while our symbols keep us safely distant from our embodied selves. But certain situations – illness, pain, risky libidinal misadventure, and also simply a cessation of wanting to exist – emphasize this inescapable intimacy. No luxury, purchase or symbolic conversion can occur when this desiring relation emerges. The desire for death returns to being the pre-symbolic need, just as one needs sustenance, in certain circumstances. From the exterior, these circumstances may seem tragic but there is no room for the luxury of lamentation for the intimate who wishes to die. Imagine the promise of eating them as a euthanizing mercy. And then we find the social contract intervenes where it least belongs – into the freedom to choose not how or what to be but simply whether to be. When living becomes unbearable, the affirmation of life comes in the form of the freedom and capacity to open an alternative, which happens to be death, to be eaten, to be the necrophile's beloved, to be food for the nonhuman's supper. Death here is not nihilism or failure but the only available creative outlet in an impossible situation. Death here is an affirmation of life and ethics, because it is welcoming the natural contract that the social contract denies. The social contract owns our life from birth to death. The transgression of self-death is identical to the ethics of available freedom to open a new direction to the cosmos by adapting a cosmological point of view where we are simply a tiny part of a greater inexhaustible mesh of connections (without hierarchy or form as in religion). This cosmology is life as a phenomenon in no need of meaning or qualification and our ability to see ourselves as part of that system underpins why death should be available also without qualification to those who seek it.

The queer politics of death activism

Considering that originally queer sexuality was defined purely by the incapacity to reproduce (an asinine and unverifiable schema already), queer sexuality is both a desire borne of cessation of reproduction (death to the species) and a desire which inevitably leads to unnatural (plethora within nature but illicit within the social contract) participations that are hyper-productive. What is produced is chimera, hybrid, unseen newness because the partner terms coming together are unique combinations. This makes human reproduction inherently anti-queer and the production of all art inherently queer. Reproduction is production of the same. As lodgers upon the earth, humans are awful. Everyone knows that. Many movements from VHEMT to the Church of Euthanasia to efilism to ecosophical theory and general antinatalism agree that humans acting like humans are violating and destroying any examples of life that don't conform or benefit the model of the Vitruvian Man. Why reproduce the same in the hope of difference when we can produce difference guaranteed through ahuman becomings found in arts, hybrid politics, collectives and all groups which don't demand verisimilitude of being a certain kind of human in order to count? The cessation of the human species doesn't mean death for anyone except this kind of verisimilitude. The adaptation to a ceasing species does require the death of the politics of sameness which is currently corroding the planet. What is more radical and effective than collectives who express with polyvocality and who don't need to be identical to desire collectively? The death of identity itself in a move towards the death of the human is a goal shared with art as it involves infinite and infinitesimal imagination, unnatural interkingdom participations, argument not to be won but as genesis of mediated newness, thought as a means of opening portals, not as an imposable structure. Every project, every day, every moment becomes political, artistic and catalyst for change by virtue of the shared commitment to death of identity and dominant humanity, without requiring conformity. This is the ethics of affect, the simple openness to express and allow others to express towards creating n directions which remap the potentialities of the world.

The personhood and simultaneous abjection bestowed on a corpse is an absurdity worthy of an artistic practice. So as art as activism is driven by love, we should be embracing alternate uses for human corpses, from fuel to food to fetishes that can alleviate mourning. We parasites at the table must become the feast that we are destined to be, without denial. 'Respecting' the corpse perpetuates anthropocentrism beyond death: 'I consider him to be a parasite in the political sense, in that a human group is organized with one way relations, where one eats the other and where the second cannot benefit at all from the first' (Serres 2005: 5). The parasite's meal for Serres starts as abuse until it becomes common usage. What we do, our voracious insatiable anthropocentrism is abuse of the world. The squeamish thought of 'abusing' a corpse is simply squeamishness. Nature does not see it as abuse. Only the social. Nature would see it as parasite become host. Nature would call it love:

> The feast of love then can be celebrated, gathering together the mortal and the divine, the earthly and the celestial in an encounter where giving and receiving are exchanged in the elation of the present. This present provides the bridge between the past and future insofar as it retains the perceived attraction in order to make it a gift to the other, while adapting this giving to the memory of the other, and insofar as the present consents to receive what the other will offer and what will result as blessings from the feast celebrated together. (Irigaray 2002: 131)

As humans cease their reproduction to open the world to the other, to make way for the nonhuman and environments at the table, embracing death shows us there is nothing to fear in our own meaninglessness. The duration of our lives can be a duration of care of all lives based on both the inevitable and creative connections we make. We humans will leave leftovers, and in order to care for the leftover mess we have created, novel ways of thinking how those leftovers can become useful for the others at the table are as much a part of care for the world as no longer occupying it. There is no meaning to our lives, there is nothing eternal in our deaths, but this does not preclude us from making the lives we lead ones that care for the world and care for the connections, distant and near, acknowledged and secret, that allow the potentia of nonhumans and environments to proliferate by our becoming host in our absence and by our leftovers.

6

The future in the age of the Apocalypse

Every age has its impending apocalypse. Every arena has its intimate apocalypse. Every understanding of the present has the apocalypses upon which it reflects and those which it sees as imminent. The end of the world shows us two highly postmodern 'things' – life, time, history and existence are neither narrative nor linear, and a thing's thingness is made up of its own mythology, not empirical truth. Like, art, like occulture, mythology hinges to truth as a mechanism of affect, so there is always truth in the impetus to activism whether or not there is in the cause. We occupy a world where the unexpected affects of anthropocentric causes, primarily industrial, evince how very little we know even when we think we know. Nonhuman animals, especially farmed or those enslaved for entertainment, are born into their own kind of apocalypse where their misery is sealed and their end nigh as the very purpose of their birth. Current feminist movements are interrogating the sexist apocalypse women are born into, where assault from a young age is expected, rather than an aberrance. Each minoritarian set is similarly born into their own kind of apocalypse, various microcosmic holocausts, while the anthropocene watches and fears the great, single apocalypse that will wipe us all out. It is the concept of this 'us' that is the problem. What would be so terrible to be wiped out of a world which many already negotiate as dystopic at best and post-apocalyptic at worst? Is the idea that we are not already within the apocalypse a luxurious one, and always has been for anyone not privileged enough to be within a certain economic, gendered and racial percentile? If the world is dystopic, why fear an apocalypse? It seems a thoroughly Western fetish borne of fear of losing the accursed share which makes us selfish and miserable. This may account for the continued popularity of biblical apocalypse analyses even in contemporary apocalyptic studies, from the mythologizing proselytizing of luxuriating priests to the mythologizing proselytizing of luxuriating capitalist panicking consumers perhaps – whether living in a bunker or living on credit. But the marauding demons are also humans and the four archangels of Revelation also the Four Horsemen of the Apocalypse. I guess that would make the Antichrist nature itself, a very sad victor utterly extinguished of power by its parasites. The ahuman is not part of the anthropocene's 'us' – it is humans who want to forsake human privilege. The disappearance of most or all of the world's human population, whether slowly and volitionally, or as the result of an environmental series of events, lacks the catastrophic tones of the fear of the apocalypse beloved of theology, science fiction and disaster films because increasingly when we ask the value of being a human if it means holding a violent dominion over other life and the earth, the value of human disappearance becomes more benevolent, attractive and gets to the heart of the divide between life at any cost and the durational experience of living as a quality. The 'us' of the anthropocene may be the final moment of equality, because we are all going to die. Mary Manjikian states, 'By virtue of its very existence, the apocalyptic novel puts forth the claim that "it is possible that in the future my nation will not prevail. It is possible that instead we will fail – and that in the grand scheme of history, all of our accomplishments will come to mean very little as we ourselves will"' (2012: 100). What humans have accomplished in art has been truly exceptional. *For* humans. What humans have accomplished for the world is questionable at best and devastating more pragmatically. The ridiculously narcissistic question of what we will mean to the future is part of breeder rhetoric that perpetuates a species which cannot guarantee that their offspring will be anything more than future parasites on an assaulted world. If there is such a simple binary as success and failure, then the human and its age of the anthropocene have failed. Why does collective or mass death terrify anthropocentrism? Why do those who proselytize the apocalypse always exempt themselves from its wrath? How can the future be thought when we both fear and already occupy the apocalypse? How can we cease to fail the earth?

The role of art in activism stands as a foil to the increasing rigid right wing politics of even middle governments. Where the activism of human extinction sounds like an apocalyptic vision, its slowness, care and creativity directly insults the restrictions of fascism, of which anthropocentrism is a clear version, which creates an apocalypse of thought. The 'us' that we are so afraid will end is unification with the enemy of the earth. That us is repudiated by minoritarian politics and the ahuman. Foucault, in defining fascism, states, in the second of his seven tenets for an anti-fascist manual, 'Develop action, thought and desires by proliferation, juxtaposition and disjunction, and not by subdivision and pyramidal hierarchization' (1983: xiii). The entities we are must proliferate in ahuman becomings to become traitor to our species, disjunctive to the natural world for which we care, but caring nonetheless. Each of us can remember an apocalypse, or more, that we have lived through – many of us remember learning to deal with nuclear war in horrific documentaries we watched in classrooms, the AIDS crisis, and now we are told variously that we have as little as twelve years left (see Watts 2018) before the world as we know it will change. At the time of writing, the United Kingdom is about to undergo its own Brexit apocalypse showing that fascism can and does win, while Brazil's new right-wing president Jair Bolsonaro is the first in a generation to see the indigenous people and their rainforest environments as a liability rather than protected (while also setting back women's rights under the same minister). There are apocalypses, large and small, for every age. What these three relatively arbitrary examples show is that the apocalypse is at this moment in time, going mainstream. There seems to be something deathbound and deeply fatalistic about these three examples. This fatalism insinuates, covert to the ahuman's celebration of death, that certain anthropocentric agents covet the most detrimental and grim deaths they can squeeze out of what is left of this exhausted earth and its occupants, with the usual victims at the frontline. These examples are not unto themselves apocalyptic because they lack the wholesale annihilation, the end of days promises, but they are the molecular apocalypses that become incremental until the trajectories they advocate atrophy into a kind of normality. But the liberal world is similarly apocalyptic. In the in-fighting that is always anthropocentric and cares little for the third party of biogea, the left remains concerned with the self and the other as a reflection or impending fate of the self – whether it is saving the future for the children, or for a sense of smug social justice that has become currency over action. I would identify breeding and identity politics as the precise points where left politics forsakes the earth for anthropocentrism. While self and the imagined offspring remain privileged, or even viable, there can be no place for biogea. The minor apocalypse examples above are also reactions to what humans see as an unfurling apocalypse – wild nature must be tamed, plundered and exhausted in the social contract; we must 'take back' the phantasy of anthropocentric hierarchy which difference politics and philosophy excavates as always already a white masculine ideal of dominance for all who 'pass'. Even the environmental catastrophes our anthropocentric practices have caused are styled as 'nature fighting back'. We refuse accountability if it means the end of our luxurious control. The ethics of difference that semi anti-anthropocentric philosophies have explored, from feminism and anti-racism to more contemporary anti-speciesism, already heralded the apocalypse of the dominant human whose dominance was entirely arbitrary and was anything but evenly distributed, even based on this perceived fulfilment of the criteria of being the right colour and gender. The social contract's favoured technique of pitting the corporeally dominant white male populace against the minoritarian instead of their mirror images in power has led to the rise of both the right and the reification of non-dominant identities as a sort of necessary evil in addressing social justice. But it's always social. Never natural. Lyotard, in a beautiful analysis of Orwell's *1984*, demarcates the ways in which there are two postmodern trajectories that are shared by art and theory but better expressed in art because it writes without claiming to direct. These are bureaucratic power and love. Totalitarianism relies on written legislation, and, after Serres, this would suggest that all social contracts across all epistemes are totalitarian, at least in their anthropocentrism. By this, the apocalypse has always been the immanent state of being for nonhumans and environments. Lyotard identifies one exception to the abstract written that is totalitarianism's technique: love. Love belongs to the sensible, the corporeal, the visceral, and, most importantly, love belongs to the deprivileging of the single point of view that this manifesto would call anthropocentric totalitarianism. He states,

> And in this [social] contact, love is the exception. It demands the permeability and the surrender of my field of perspective to yours. Hence the never-ending search for a different idiom of sensibility, this vertigo where my idiom and yours falter, where they look for exchange, where they resist and discover each other. (1992: 92)

In this understanding, any limiting politics is already apocalyptic, because it ends time, ends expansion, ends the oscillation or proliferation of perspectives. The social contract as ubiquitous legislation between humans but affecting the earth is potestas in denial of the potentia of the ahuman and the natural.

For me personally, I am deeply saddened that there has never managed to be an annihilation of the human species, in spite of plague and war, the latter seeming the ultimately ironic kind of self-serving apocalypse showing the absolute idiocy of the human being the pinnacle of the pyramid of life. While the earth is in the grip of the apocalypse the anthropocene delivers, humans fear an apocalypse that our consumerism, our greed and our narcissism welcomes. The apocalypse will not come with an explosive bang or a diluvian wave but with apathy and internalized despair, and a few victors to whom will go some wretched spoils. Winning a desolate earth in a plush bunker seems more important than a life spent in dissolution caring for the other lives on the earth, be they a final generation of parentless children (the orphan is rarely coveted by the breeder), dissymmetrically challenged global areas of all organisms or the left-over generations of nonhumans enslaved for pets, on farms, circuses and other incarcerations. There is a project of care in embracing human extinction. It is neither fast nor eruptive, neither murderous of other humans (eugenic or indiscriminate) nor fetishistic of a future or eternity at the expense of immanent lived experiences by and of the other. The liberation of the world is not the romance of an inconceivable hyperobject made aesthetic as Morton suggests (2013: 108) when it is taken out of the anthropocentric eye of aestheticization for self-gratification. Rather, the abstract vastness, inconceivability and imperceptibility of the world is precisely that which reminds us that we have the dubious honour of being utterly inconsequential in a meaningful way (by meaningful, I mean as a productive part of a disparate assemblage known as ecology) and utterly murderous in an anthropocentric way. Our inconsequentiality as meaningful from a cosmic perspective embraces the occulture of Lovecraft without the nihilism–hedonism or existential angst of the majoritarian. Simultaneous with acknowledging we likely were and will never be of any objectively measurable importance in anthropocentric history, like the anti-fascist activist we also adhere to finite territories of activism, exploiting what we can do that, to a nonhuman animal or another organism, may be very meaningful indeed. The end of the overvaluation of individual human subjectivity is absolutely necessary for this kind of care to be produced and this kind of activist imagination to be catalysed as it directly antagonizes the techniques of the self that capitalism produces and fascism demands. Foucault calls the loss of subjectivity, far from a form of psychosis, the opening towards a healing, towards becoming animal, vegetal, mineral (1983: xxii). There is care in loss of self and loss of the human species, for humans and for nonhumans. For Guattari, this begins with the apocalypse of the individual as ego, as self, and we can extend that to as species:

The principle specific to mental ecology is that its approach to existential territories is that it derives from a pre-objectal and pre-personal logic of the sort that Freud has described as being a 'primary process'. One could call this the logic of the 'included middle', in which black and white are indistinct, where the beautiful coexists with the ugly, the inside with the outside, the 'good' object with the 'bad' ... in the particular case of the ecology of the phantasm, each attempt to locate it cartographically requires the drafting of an expressive framework that is both singular, and more precisely, singularized. Gregory Bateson has clearly shown that what he calls the 'ecology of ideas' cannot be contained within the psychology of the individual, but organizes itself into 'systems' or minds, the boundaries of which no longer coincide with the participant individuals. (2000: 54)

Guattari's statement on the relationship between the ecology of the individual and of activism here has many affiliations with and vitalistic adaptations towards the apocalypse, both the one in which we are living and human extinction. Guattari's attention to the pre-symbolic as accessed by the adult, what he calls the asemiotic and from whence the inspiration for my coining the concept of the ahuman comes, shows a double apocalypse. The first is that there is no self, either born or developed, no ego that accesses some singular uniqueness within a transcendental metaphysical individuality that would return us to Descartes. There is nothing special about the human organism when it is born because it thinks nothing a priori, so it never existed and thus cannot face its own apocalypse. The territories of capital, state, religion and family constitute the individual as they develop, so the idea of free will and individuality again is challenged by what I would term the apocalyptic nature of signifying regimes, those linguistic and representational systems that close off and delimit the mucosal, leaky affects of all encounters. Signification, or at least interpretation, may even be the apocalypse of affect, which would make anthropocentrism the destroyer of ethical accountability. Guattari accesses Spinoza by defining an individual as an expressive framework, one which is also affected. The in-between of the in-between beloved of chaos magick is invoked here – Guattari's included middle. The individual is a cartography of included middles between and constituted by material expressions and affectations. As a species, if the human is the apex of the pyramid, the ahuman could become the included middle of the care of the world while we diminish – no longer the species which demands dominion but attendant to our winding down presence and the affects they produce within the inevitable assemblages with the natural in which we find ourselves. Humans would no longer be life as humans, 'human life' as a demarcated ontological object, but living for the natural, living as an included middle between a biogea whose future we would not seek to be a part of through continued reproduction of the species. The human could be the temporal included middle of the history of time rather than the definition of history itself. The twilight of man, like the dawn of man, the included middle of expanses beyond us. Within this cosmic eternal is the very real activism Guattari proposes in attaching tactically to drafts of activism. Capitalist and neoliberal activisms love the pay-off, the immediate gratification, the worthy victim, the speciesist hierarchy, the racialized child. Activism territories of the included middle neither designates before the encounter nor evaluates after. The encounter is the activism of immanence, so the future itself in immanent activism at a direct level is present, and the idea of futurity faces its apocalypse. Clearly working for and within territories that do not announce their value through aligning with a pre-formed binary table of good and bad, pretty and ugly, makes the desiring project of care a queer one. Queering activism goes far beyond any form of gender or species queering towards a repudiation of all taxonomical borders. In a winding down of the earth and our duty of care to life, we may very well find ourselves caring for some unpalatable territories occupied by lives personally apprehended as deplorable. This is the point where the included middle makes relation incandesce as the privileged site(s) of the territory. Ecosophy, by emphasizing, like Spinozan ethics, relation over individuals as objects and/or subjects, takes government, group and combat from care. It takes dissymmetry from care though it attends to different levels of access within relations without making value unbalanced. Pragmatically, it also denies the futurity rhetoric utilized by heteronormative conservativism to procure votes and deny alterities of all varieties critiqued by anti-reproduction theorists such as Lee Edelman (2004) and Penelope Deutcher (2017).

Why does the ahuman apocalypse, slow and careful as it is, have to be so extreme? Margrit Shildrik writes of disability, 'The productive ruse is that as long as happiness remains a phantasm, just out of reach – which in the context of debility and slow death is almost inevitable – then the interminable quest for it can yield profit' (2015: 17). The earth is not such an abstract hyperobject that its imperceptibility prevents us from acting towards its endurance. But the sustainability argument perpetuates this image of a disabled earth that reprioritizes the individual and small acts of personal smugness which capitalize on the possibility we can sustain our lives, these excessive and destructive lives, that in turn create industries out of charities and charity as consumer action out of radical activism. There is no denying that the activisms presented here are extreme. But isn't anything less perpetuating the debilitated earth argument that keeps individuals and their closest alikes in a bubble of self-satisfaction and self-perpetuation punctuated by occasional acts that, rather than being gracious, attain more value in announcing them on social media than in their material affects? The arguments against climate change on a political scale are mirrored in those who claim that not reproducing or not being malzoan are against their individual rights to choose. These are the same argument structures used by white power hate groups, men's rights activists and any other manner of structure where individual liberty eradicates even the vaguest flawed semblance of equality for a pseudo-nostalgic return to might-is-right majoritarian hedonism. The mainstreaming of these structures, which are, of course, perennial and far from infrequent, may be a sign that for the minoritarian, the apocalypse seems closer than ever, and so the backlash is more vitriolic, more infantile. Philosophically, the cessation of the human is (somewhat hilariously) an actual and discursive creation of a relation between traditional ethics, both from a moral philosophy view (including utilitarianism, but as ahumanism is anti-speciesist, we count all organisms) and Kantian or Hegelian dialectics, and the burgeoning field of feminist ethics which renders the denigrated aspects of so-called femininity as crucial in the creation of relational ethical activisms. The latter is, of course, already more aligned with Spinozist, Nietzschean and Continental post-structuralism, but the concept of care seems to be one uniquely feminist in current writing. Daryl Koehn states,

Male ethics stress deductive reasoning as the hallmark of ethical reasoning. These ethics would have us derive our duties from the Kantian categorical imperative, from a state of nature, or from some other original position. While female ethicists do argue for their ethic, they highlight the importance that imagination plays in our ability to relate to our fellow human beings and in our characterization of the various practical problems and choices we daily confront. In particular, imagination plays a large role in the female ethics' virtues of care, trust, and empathy, all virtues (or quasi-virtues) largely overlooked by previous ethics. Female ethicists think that we should not assume away difference by positing a typical community member. For female ethicists, the ethical and political problem is largely one of achieving sufficient imaginative insight into the perspectives of persons with experiences and commitments different from our own to be able to undertake joint actions and to form mutually beneficial relations. By repressing difference, male ethics assume away the ethical problem. (1998: 8)

While what Koehn writes may seem obvious at this point, it raises some concerns regarding what the apocalypse means, or, more precisely, to whom the apocalypse means the apocalypse. The concept of community embraces relationality, but, as Koehn emphasizes, that community also presumes sameness. The use of imagination, along with the other aspects of female ethics she advocates, including relationality of the self with others, valuation of difference, care for the vulnerable, world-changing (such as activism) and breakdown of public and private, all dismantle the cult of the individual, which begins from the cultivation of individual identity and continues to living the longest life at any cost. The former begins with the rhetoric of the enforcement of a belief that the self is unique and special, while nurturing it with false consciousness and combative preservation at the expense of all else. The duration of life extends these tendencies variously until the activist or the abolitionist or the antinatalist finds themselves designated as abject, along with the unapologetic rapists and criminals, traitors which Kristeva uses as exemplars of abjection (1982: 4). But the activist doesn't care because the basic tenet of ethical activism is fighting without identity. So the very premise of an activist is antagonistic to the logic of identity which founds the possibility (but not the potential) of being a being. This positions the individual, the majoritarian, the malzoan, the privileged, face to face with the potential for their own apocalypse by looking at the human who fights for the other. The pyramid is reversed. The apex, instead of consuming and exploiting the entire pyramid, now holds it upon their shoulders and waits to be crushed. This weight is activism and it is joy, because, like art, it is the apocalypse that requires not an end but an infinite imagining of beginnings beyond the individual. It is a gift of artistic necessity placed on all humans. The question becomes, With what intensities will we meet the apocalypse? It definitely need not be a terrible experience or the sudden catastrophic event we are told will arrive. It certainly does involve an afterlife, but not for humans. It takes the end away from religious judgement or primordial post-apocalyptic desperation. But it also is an 'I do not know' because obviously the diminishment and care involved in rethinking the need for humans on the earth will be both spatially and temporally highly metamorphic and adaptive. It simply involves a combination of hitherto bifurcated intensities – active listening, empowered grace, autonomous passivity. Care is a logic. Care is an ethic. And Spinoza's demand for potentia over potestas means care is independent of an overarching single structure of action that can be imposed on all life and all situations and relations.

'You will recognize a thinker based on the way he [*sic*] goes from truth to possibilities. As life goes from repetition to negentropy' (Serres 1997: 17). Serres addresses the chaos necessary to shift life from repetition to negentropy; this chaos is harnessed in the faith and hope which ahumanism requires of humans that their own extinction is both viable and vital. Bernard Stiegler states,

What is the meaning of *belief* when, for example, we say that we *no longer believe* it is possible to change a situation in which the 'human factor' that we now refer to as 'anthropogenic' is, if not a cosmic element, then at least a geo-logical one, and when we *do not believe* that it is possible to change human behaviour? And *what is the relationship here between believing, wanting and individuating?* What *positivity* can we fashion from this *negative belief*, that is, this negative protention? How might we fight against it without making the mistake of denying its legitimacy, that is, without denying how serious the situation really is? Such negative protention is inherently *performative and self-fulfilling*. (2018: 6, original emphases)

Only an anthropocentric evaluation of the claims and demands made in this manifesto would see the human apocalypse as negative, as performative (surely she can't be *serious?*), as ultimately a manifesto advocating for death. The Neganthropocene belongs to the anthropocene, while Stiegler suggests that this today can belong to something else entirely:

very singularly in the today of today – today as *never before* – *only by default*, only *by the default*, as the default, and as *the new stage of a différance that remains to be made* in and after what is called the Anthropocene. Thought [*pensée*] can today be only what we could therefore call, *on the condition* that we write it, and as that which thus refers to différ(a)nce, *the experience of thinking about and taking care of* [*p(a)nser*] how the absence of epoch must, as a last resort, constitute not a 'new epoch' but rather *another epokhality,* which would come to *think treatment* [*pansements*] *otherwise,* that is, cares, that is, illness and health … Let us call the Neganthropocene the possibility of what presents itself firstly as impossibility, which is to say, as wholly other – as *a wholly other era.* (2018: 233–4, original emphases)

Stiegler locates hope in a philosophical realm, asking us to reinject thought into what we have hitherto claimed is our knowledge of, for example, Nietzsche (vital epokhality) and Hegel (neganthropocentric, hubristic). The ahuman situates material commitments to seemingly impossible acts (to be fair, they are not that impossible; there are millions of abolitionist antinatalists in the world). Both share the traditionally feminist but essentially antianthropocentric quality of care, and after Serres, we see that care increasingly comes to be aligned with thinking the unthinkable in order to create a new epoch. The nexus of activism occurs at the point where the final binary of the impossible with the possible is collapsed. We are faced with the impossible, as every thinker of every age has also faced, and we will commit to acting upon it nonetheless, even though to do so requires the embrace of yet another apocalypse – that of causal signifying systems. The structure of such systems, which manifest truth (but not the 'true'), judicial knowledge, science, state, religion and family, the enemies of the natural contract and historically the enemies of minoritarians, is what structures the possibility of a possibility. And that structure says ahuman calls to activism are absurd. But it serves only the anthropocene, so these calls are not only possible as potentials but also are increasingly easy, especially for those privileged enough to have access to reproductive rights and nutritious food on a practical level, and the freedom to practice artistry of any and all kinds within our realms. These 'short forms of closure' (Noyer 2016: 99), as Jean-Max Noyer calls collective assemblages of actants (of varying species and qualities), are trendy in transhuman theory as they perpetuate self-serving systems of their own being. Utilizing short closures to evoke entropy and chaotic perturbations creates new systems that could be unimaginable or unrecognizable. Nothing need be lost, just changed, as the chaotic cosmic world of post-apocalyptic monsters sees our materiality transform.

'With thy love, go into thine isolation, my brother, and with thy creating; and late only will justice limp after thee. With my tears, go into thine isolation, my brother. I love him who seeketh to create beyond himself, and thus succumbeth' (Nietzsche 1997: 61). Thus spake Zarathustra. I have persistently used the pronoun 'we' in *The Ahuman Manifesto*. This has no doubt been both frustrating and irritating for the reader; it certainly was for the students, academics and general public who were presented early versions of some of the work. No one, it seemed, wished to be aligned with me, nor indeed with the selves of themselves I offered as they (as malzoans, as natalists/breeders, as majoritarians) or we (as humans together). I, who dislike my species yet heed the maxim of Zarathustra that forces one to love what one disdains in order to access creativity, to create a 'we' both scolded and celebrated from various collectives, those who are tempted historically to be defined by their allotted portion of injustice, those who are adamantly majoritarian and therefore seemingly without redemption but also enslaved by the system that enables them, both versions of the human Zarathustra critiques. The ahuman seeks to transcend anthropocentrism on a basic and material level, but at no point can I/we deny complicity with all systems. And at no point can I/we say that there is nothing to be done, nothing I/we can do. Deleuze and Guattari ask, 'But who is this we, which is not me?' (1981: 266) The we that is the collective apparatuses of the self unknown to self that make the self alien to its potentia, the unified global human species to which one is relegated and with which one is made complicit because, as one of the most often cited quotes of recent times attests (and whose origin remains in dispute, but no matter): 'Someone once said that it is easier to imagine the end of the world than to imagine the end of capitalism. We can now revise that and witness the attempt to imagine capitalism by way of imagining the end of the world' (Jameson 2003). Religion has always found it easier to imagine the end of the world than the end of whatever its acolytes do not like, whether it be as diverse as rampant sin, crop-destroying drought or Babylonian equality for minoritarians. What end-of-days prophets show is that it is easier to imagine the end of the world than almost anything, that the diluvian cleanse makes acting and being an agent of change no longer the responsibility of this 'we' that is not me, both the internally despairing conflicted actant self or the collective activism group. Maybe there is a way to save humans and reintegrate them. Maybe there is a way to resolve anthropocentrism with the natural contract. But this 'we' that is me sees the apocalypse of the nonhuman animal other as happening from the very purposeful birth of the other until their designated death, and the resolution of the human species through cessation of reproduction a compassionate and viable apocalypse but also one aligned with Zarathustra's message of creativity and creating beyond oneself. How can a philosopher be an activist or an artist without seeing beyond oneself, ending the tired self-absorbed questions that create the foundation of arid ontology, which always end up asking different versions of the same anthropocentric questions – why are we here? How can we live forever? What is the meaning of life? Perhaps metaphysical questions are apocalyptic because they are immeasurable and unanswerable yet continue to posit the possibility of being answered only in order to veil the real question that the human asks to themselves, which is no question at all but a demand for proof that they are the most special, meaningful and perfect incarnation of existence. It has always been tedious, but the more real materiality is concealed by the hypnosis of media messages of consumerism which are frighteningly mimetic of fascist romances of the real as a dreamlike state to conceal the brutality of what it takes to sustain any totalitarian machine, the more selfish and awful the anthropocene seems. This manifesto has spoken of hope and faith, in a different kind of apocalypse of the anthropocene, but belief remains tricky. We ahumans are asked to believe in the unbelievable – humans can end, activism can make the lives of other organisms bearable and even joyful, but the world we live in now is unbelievable. Any moment of any day we meet the events of the world with disbelief. Disbelief at anthropocentric hubris, at what passes for 'ethical' behaviour, often in the name of sustainability, resolution of crisis or some other pathetic display of the anthropocene pretending to care. Our world is already one where the real has experienced the apocalypse. It cannot be underestimated how many lives are living in a post-apocalyptic world right at this moment, *because* of human effects *and human will*.

What are we afraid of? It is astonishing how many slow apocalypse artworks, literature, films and television, which include the fin–de–siècle horrors from H. G. Wells to Lovecraft, atomic-age monstrous mutant animals, and, in contemporary times, zombies and invading aliens, have at their core the simple message, 'What would it feel like to be treated as humans treat nonhumans?' In a perverse inversion of teratology, we are the monsters. The hypocrisy of catharsis achieved through watching others treat us how we treat others is as despair-inducing as it is poignant. We are afraid of being treated how the anthropocene treats every aspect of the earth.

What are we afraid of? We know we cannot live forever. We know death is the most banal and certain quality of being born. Yet we covet transhumanism, religious afterlives, eternal reincarnations or living on through our art or our children. We do not care for the present. We fear death with more fascination than we live life. The cessation of the human species denies no one the life they have, so what are we afraid of? We are afraid we are not as special as we think we are.

What are we afraid of? We are afraid we won't have lived enough, 'got' enough, consumed enough, been free to experience the fleeting life we have. Immanent experience in capitalism has converted pleasure to measure and desire to a dialectic so mechanized that we are striving to be equal to inanimate luxury objects even while claiming to be superior to sentient nonhumans. We are worthy. You're worth it. Seeing ethical consumption as denial is far more repudiative of the reality of murder, torture and enslavement than the simulacrum of lies which demand that only through our choice to consume what we want will we know and design ourselves as agents. Otherwise, we are just subject to restrictions that limit our 'pleasure', pleasure born entirely of a tradition of violence without reflection.

What are we afraid of? We are afraid that by foregrounding the abstract earth and the occupants with which we cannot clearly communicate, the oppressed with whom we can communicate will be forgotten before they have been recognized. Cessation of humans resolves literally all human on human oppression. Care demands that we distribute value absolutely equally. This is a deviating tactic that exhumes the corpse of identity, especially 'What about me?'. Ahuman activism refuses all hierarchy, which means all incremental welfare politics of this first, then this, or better is better than nothing.

What are we afraid of? Activism is hard because there is no plan. This is something indeed that can cause fear because activism as a heterogenous chaosmosis 'does not constitute a translucent, indifferent zone of being, but an intolerable nucleus of ontological creationism' (Guattari 1995: 83). Intolerable to the anthropocentric, perhaps. Frightening to the attentive radical who wants to reterritorialize finite areas *and* to the human who adheres to the established cartographies of possibility imposed from above. This fear is a gift. It makes artists of us all as a way out of anthropocentrism, giving us the tools of imagination and creativity and the potentials of each body and collection of bodies being capable of expressions that can cause affects entirely because of their difference rather than challenged due to difference. This is a luxury fear. It is understandable, but none of us can see the future with transparency, so all action is destined to be included within this fear. In this moment, and tactically better is better than nothing, because it is difference not on the terms of the anthropocene, which is where welfare arguments arise, but on ahuman terms.

With tears and love and joy. Be afraid. But we can still act.

REFERENCES

Adams, Carol J. (1990), *The Sexual Politics of Meat*, London: Continuum.

Adams, Carol J. (1995), *Neither Man nor Beast: Feminism and the Defense of Animals*, New York: Continuum.

Adams, Carol J. (2009), 'Post-Meateating', in Tom Tyler and Manuela Rossini (eds), *Animal Encounters*, 45–72, Leiden: BRILL.

Adams, Carol J. (2014), 'The War on Compassion', in Patricia MacCormack (ed.), *The Animal Catalyst: Towards Ahuman Theory*, 15–26, London: Bloomsbury.

Ahmed, Sara (2017), *Living a Feminist Life*, Durham: Duke University Press.

Alcoff, Linda Martin, and Mohanty, Satya P. (2006), 'Reconsidering Identity Politics', in Linda Martin Alcoff, Michael Hames-Garcia, Satya P. Mohanty and Paula M. L. Moya (eds), *Identity Politics Reconsidered*, 1–9, New York: Palgrave Macmillan.

Andrade, Oswald de (1991), 'Cannibalist Manifesto', trans. Leslie Bary, *Latin American Literary Review*, 19 (38) (Jul.–Dec.): 38–47.

Arendt, Hannah (1964), *On Revolution*, London: Penguin.

Bahna-Jones, Tara Sophia (2011), 'The Art of Truth Telling', in Lisa Kemmerer (ed.), *Sister Species: Women, Animals and Social Justice*, 117–26, Urbana: University of Illinois Press.

Ball, Hugo (1996), *Flight Out of Time: A Dada Diary*, trans. Ann Raimes, Berkeley: University of California Press.

Bataille, Georges (1962), *Eroticism*, trans. Mary Dalwood, London: Penguin.

Beistegui, Miguel De (2015), 'Desire within and beyond Biopolitics', in Miguel De Beistegui, Giuseppe Bianco and Marjorie Gracieuse (eds), *The Care of Life: Transdisciplinary Perspectives in Bioethics and Biopolitics*, 241–60, London: Rowman & Littlefield.

Bellegarrigue, Anselme (2002), *The World's First Anarchist Manifesto*, London: The Kate Sharpley Library.

Benatar, David (2008), *Better Never to Have Been: The Harm of Coming into Existence*, Oxford: Oxford University Press.

Benhabib, Seyla (1992), *Situating the Self: Gender, Community and Postmodernism in Contemporary Ethics*, Cambridge: Polity Press.

Bifo Berardi, Franco (2015), *Heroes*, London: Verso.

Braidotti, Rosi (2010), 'On Putting the Active back into Activism', *New Formations: Deleuzian Politics?* 68: 42–57.

Braidotti, Rosi (2012), *The Posthuman*, Cambridge: Polity.

Breeze Harper, A. (2010), *Sistah Vegan*, Brooklyn: Lantern Books.

Breton, Andrè (1969), *Manifestoes of Surrealism*, trans. Richard Seaver and Helen R. Lane, Ann Arbor: University of Michigan Press.

Campbell, Matt (2018), 'Satanic Temple Again Challenges Missouri Abortion Laws on Religious Grounds', *The Kansas City Star*, 6 March. Available online: https://www.kansascity.com/news/article203702319.html (accessed 6 July 2019).

Carrington, Damian (2018), 'Humans Just 0.01% of All Life but Have Destroyed 83% of Wildlife', *The Guardian*, 21 May. Available online: https://www.theguardian.com/environment/2018/may/21/human-race-just-001-of-all-life-but-has-destroyed-over-80-of-wild-mammals-study (accessed 6 July 2019).

Carroll, Peter (1987), *Liber Null and Psychonaut*, York Beach, ME: Weiser.

Cavendish, Roger (1970–3), *Man, Myth and Magic*, 24 Volume Encyclopaedia Set, Leeds: Purnell and Sons.

Charles, R. H. (2003), *The Book of Enoch the Prophet*, York Beach, ME: Weiser.

Church of Euthanasia, http://www.churchofeuthanasia.org/.

Colebrook, Claire (2009), 'On the Very Possibility of Queer Theory', in Chrysanthi Nigianni and Merl Storr (eds), *Deleuze and Queer Theory*, 11–23, Edinburgh: Edinburgh University Press.

Colebrook, Claire (2018), 'Extinction', in Rosi Braidotti and Maria Hlavajova (eds), *Posthuman Glossary*, 150–3, London: Bloomsbury.

Craddock, Ida (2017), *Heavenly Bridegrooms, Psychic Wedlock, The Heaven of the Bible, The Wedding Night, Right Marital Living and Other Papers on Marriage and Sex*, City Not Known: McAllister Editions.

Crenshaw, Kimberlè (2019), *On Intersectionality*, New York: New Press.

Crowley, Aleister (1991), *Magick without Tears*, Tempe, AZ: Falcon Press.

Davidson, Gustav (1967), *A Dictionary of Angels*, New York: Simon & Schuster.

Davis, Heather, and Turpin, Etienne (2015), 'Art and Death: Lives Between the Fifth Assessment and the Sixth Extinction', in Heather Davis and Etienne Turpin (eds), *Art in the Anthropocene*, 3–30, London: Open Humanities Press.

Deleuze, Gilles (1988), *Spinoza: Practical Philosophy*, trans. Robert Hurley, San Francisco, CA: City Lights Books.

Deleuze, Gilles (1994), *Masochism: Coldness and Cruelty*, trans. Jean McNeil, New York: Zone Books.

Deleuze, Gilles (1999), *Foucault*, trans. Seán Hand, London: The Athlone Press.

Deleuze, Gilles (2001), *The Fold: Leibniz and the Baroque*, trans. Tom Conley, London: The Athlone Press.

Deleuze, Gilles (2006), *Nietzsche and Philosophy*, trans. Hugh Tomlinson, London: Bloomsbury.

Deleuze, Gilles, and Guattari, Félix (1981), 'How to Make Yourself a Body without Organs', trans. Suzanne Guerlac, in Francoise Péraldi (ed.), *Polysexuality*, 265–9, New York: Semiotext(e).

Deleuze, Gilles, and Guattari, Fèlix (1986), *Kafka: Toward a Minor Literature*, trans. Dana Polan, Minneapolis: University of Minnesota Press.

Deleuze, Gilles, and Guattari, Fèlix (1987), *A Thousand Plateaus: Capitalism and Schizophrenia II*, trans. Brian Massumi, London: Athlone.

Deleuze, Gilles, and Guattari, Fèlix (1994), *What is Philosophy?* trans. Hugh Tomlinson and Graham Burchell, New York: Columbia University Press.

Deutscher, Penelope (2017), *Foucault's Futures: A Critique of Reproductive Reason*, Columbia University Press.

Dunayer, Joan (2004), *Speciesism*, Derwood, ML: Ryce.

Edelman, Lee (2004), *No Future: Queer Theory and the Death Drive*, Durham, NC: Duke University Press.

Ehrenreich, Barbara, and English, Deirdre (2010), *Witches, Midwives, & Nurses: A History of Women Healers*, New York: Feminist Press at the City University of New York.

Extinction Rebellion, https://rebellion.earth/.

Faxneld, Per (2017), *Satanic Feminism: Lucifer as Liberator of Woman in Nineteenth Century Culture*, Oxford: Oxford University Press.

Federici, Silvia (2004), *Caliban and the Witch: Women, The Body and Primitive Accumulation*, Brooklyn: Autonomedia.

Federici, Silvia (2018), *Re-enchanting the World: Feminism and the Politics of Commons*, Oakland: Kairos Press.

Foucault, Michel (1983), 'Preface', in Gilles Deleuze and Fèlix Guattari (eds), *Anti-Oedipus: Capitalism and Schizophrenia*, trans. Robert Hurley, Mark Seem and Helen Lane, xi–xiv, Minneapolis: University of Minnesota Press.

Foucault, Michel (1994), 'For an Ethics of Discomfort', in James D. Faubion (ed.), *Michel Foucault: Essential Works of Foucault 1954–1984 Volume 3: Power*, 443–8, London: Penguin.

Foucault, Michel (1997), 'Thought from the Outside', trans. Brian Massumi, in Michel Foucault and Maurice Blanchot (eds), *Foucault/Blanchot*, 7–60, New York: Zone Books.

Foucault, Michel (1998), 'Preface to Transgression', in James D. Faubion (ed.), *Michel Foucault: Essential Works of Foucault 1954–1984 Volume 2: Aesthetics*, 69–88, London: Penguin.

Freud, Sigmund (1961), *Civilization and its Discontents*, trans. James Strachey, New York: Norton.

Giffney, Noreen (2009), 'Introduction', in Noreen Giffney and Michael O'Rourke (eds), *The Ashgate Research Companion to Queer Theory*, 1–16, Basingstoke: Ashgate.

Grosz, Elizabeth (1995), *Space, Time and Perversion*. Sydney: Allen and Unwin.

Guattari, Fèlix (1995), *Chaosmosis: An Ethico-Aesthetic Paradigm*, trans. Paul Bains and Julian Pefanis, Sydney: Powerhouse.

Guattari, Fèlix (1996), *Soft Subversions*, trans. David L. Sweet and Chet Wiener, New York: Semiotext(e).

Guattari, Fèlix (2000), *The Three Ecologies*, trans. Ian Pindar and Paul Sutton, London: Athlone.

Haraway, Donna (2013), *Simians, Cyborgs and Women*, London: Routledge.

Haraway, Donna (2016), *Staying with the Trouble: Making Kin in the Cthulucene*, Durham: Duke University Press.

Harman, Graham (2012), *Weird Realism: Lovecraft and Philosophy*, Hants: Zero Books.

Hawkins, Jaq D. (1996), *Understanding Chaos Magic*, Berks: Capall Bann.

Hine, Phil (1993), *Prime Chaos*, Tempe, AZ: Falcon Press.

Hine, Phil (2004), *The Pseudonomicon*, Tempe, AZ: Falcon Press.

Holert, Tom (2018), 'Art', in Rosi Braidotti and Maria Hlavajova (eds), *Posthuman Glossary*, 59–63, London: Bloomsbury.

Houellebecq, Michel (2008), *H.P. Lovecraft: Against the World, Against Life*, trans. Dorna Khazeni. London: Weidenfeld and Nicholson.

Irigaray, Luce (1985), *This Sex Which Is Not One*, trans. Catherine Porter, Ithaca: Cornell University Press.

Irigaray, Luce (1992), *Elemental Passions*, trans. Joanne Collie and Judith Still, New York: Routledge.

Irigaray, Luce (1993), *An Ethics of Sexual Difference*, trans. Carolyn Burke and Gillian C. Gill, Ithaca: Cornell University Press.

Irigaray, Luce (2002), *The Way of Love*, trans. Heidi Bostic and Stephen Pluhacek, London: Continuum.

Irigaray, Luce (2017), *To Be Born*, Cham, Switzerland: Palgrave Macmillan.

Jameson, Frederic (2003), 'Future City', *New Left Review* 21, May–June. Available online: https://newleftreview.org/II/21/fredric-jameson-future-city (accessed 6 July 2019).

Koehn, Daryl (1998), *Rethinking Feminist Ethics: Care, Trust and Empathy*, London: Routledge.

Korsgaard, Christine (2019), *Fellow Creatures: Our Obligations to the Other Animals*, Oxford: Oxford University Press.

Kramer, Samuel Noah (1972), *Sumerian Mythology: Spiritual and Literary Achievement in the Third Millennium B.C.*, Philadelphia: University of Pennsylvania Press.

Kristeva, Julia (1982), *Powers of Horror: An Essay on Abjection*, trans. Leon Roudiez, New York: Columbia University Press.

Kristeva, Julia (1991), *Strangers to Ourselves*, trans. Leon Roudiez,
  New York: Columbia University Press.

Kristeva, Julia (2002), *Revolt, She Said*, trans. Brian O'Keeffe,
  New York: Semiotext(e).

Leibniz, Gottfried Wilhelm (1995), *Philosophical Writings*, trans. Mary Morris
  and G. H. R. Parkinson. Vermont: Everyman.

Levi, Eliphas (1969), *The Key of the Mysteries*, trans. Aleister Crowley,
  London: Rider.

Levi, Eliphas (2001), *Transcendental Magic*, trans. Arthur Edward Waite, York
  Beach, ME: Weiser.

Levison, Lisa (2016), 'Coping With Animal-Cruelty Trauma', *In Defense of
  Animals*. Available online: https://www.idausa.org/coping-animal-cruelty-
  trauma/ (accessed 6 July 2019).

Lizik, Regina (2015), 'The Fatal Epidemic of Animal Care Workers That No
  One Is Talking About.' *Barkpost*. Available online: https://barkpost.com/
  compassion-fatigue-animal-workers/ (accessed 6 July 2019).

Lockwood, Alex (2018), 'Not Just What's on Your Plate: How Veganism is
  Changing the Arts' *Plant Based News*, 1 November. Available online: https://
  www.plantbasednews.org/post/not-just-whats-on-your-plate-how-veganism-
  is-changing-the-arts?fbclid=IwAR2N-H1ScOUm_ldv0YJsbFHQoM-
  Wkfk6xpjld7ItKwy5oYuozsVH2dx7yUY (accessed 6 July 2019).

Lovecraft, H. P. (1989), 'The Call of Cthulhu', *H.P. Lovecraft Omnibus 3*,
  London: Grafton.

Lovecraft, H. P. (1994), 'The Shadow Over Innsmouth', in *The Haunter of the
  Dark and Other Tales*, ed. August Derleth, 382–463, London: Harper Collins.

Lovecraft, H. P. (1999a), 'The Shadow Out of Time', *H.P. Lovecraft Omnibus 1*,
  464–544, London: Voyager.

Lovecraft, H. P. (1999b), 'Through the Gates of the Silver Key', *H.P. Lovecraft
  Omnibus 1*, 503–52, London: Voyager.

Lyotard, Jean François (1988), *The Differend: Phrases in Dispute*, trans. Georges
  Van Den Abbeele, Minneapolis: University of Minnesota Press.

Lyotard, Jean François (1992), *The Postmodern Explained*, trans. Julian Pefanis
  and Morgan Thomas, Minneapolis: University of Minnesota Press.

Lyotard, Jean Françoise (1993), *Libidinal Economy*, trans. Iain Hamilton Grant,
  London: The Athlone Press.

Lyotard, Jean-Françoise (1998), *The Assassination of Experience by Painting –
  Monory*, trans. Rachel Bowlby, London: Black Dog.

MacCormack, Patricia (2010), 'Becoming-Vulva: Flesh, Fold, Infinity', *New
  Formations: Deleuzian Politics?* 68: 93–108.

MacCormack, Patricia (2012), *Posthuman Ethics*, London: Routledge.

MacCormack, Patricia, ed. (2014), *The Animal Catalyst: Towards Ahuman Theory*, London: Bloomsbury.

MacCormack, Patricia (2017), 'Ahuman Abolition', in Patricia MacCormack and Colin Gardner (eds), *Deleuze and the Animal*, 25–36, Edinburgh: Edinburgh University Press.

Manjikian, Mary (2012), *Apocalypse and Post-Politics: The Romance of the End*. Lanham, MD: Lexington Books.

Marx, Karl, and Engels, Freidrich (2004), *The Communist Manifesto*, trans. L. M. Findlay, Peterborough, Canada: Broadview Press.

McQueen, Paddy (2015), 'Post-identity Politics and the Weightlessness of Radical Gender Theory', *Thesis Eleven*, 134 (1): 73–88.

McNay, Lois (2014), *The Misguided Search for the Political*, Cambridge: Polity Press.

Moodie, Alison (2016), 'Before you read another health study, check who's funding the research', *The Guardian*, 12 December. Available online: https://www.theguardian.com/lifeandstyle/2016/dec/12/studies-health-nutrition-sugar-coca-cola-marion-nestle (accessed 6 July 2019).

Morton, Timothy (2007), *Ecology Without Nature: Rethinking Environmental Aesthetics*, Cambridge, MA: Harvard University Press.

Morton, Timothy (2010), *The Ecological Thought*, Cambridge, MA: Harvard University Press.

Morton, Timothy (2013), *Hyperobjects: Philosophy and Ecology after the End of the World*, Minneapolis: University of Minnesota Press.

Nietzsche, Freidrich (1973), *Beyond Good and Evil*, trans. R. J. Hollingdale, London: Penguin.

Nietzsche, Freidrich (1997), *Thus Spake Zarathustra*, trans. Thomas Common, London: Wordsworth.

Nietzsche, Freidrich (2005), 'The Anti-Christ', trans. Judith Norman, in Aaron Ridley (ed.), *The Anti-Christ, Ecce Homo, Twilight of the Idols and Other Writings*, 1–68, Cambridge: Cambridge University Press.

Nigianni, Chrysanthi (2009), 'Introduction', in Chrysanthi Nigianni and Merl Storr (eds), *Deleuze and Queer Theory*, 1–10, Edinburgh: Edinburgh University Press.

Noyer, Jean-Max (2016), *Transformation of Collective Intelligences: Perspective of Transhumanism*, London: John Wiley, 2016.

O'Neill, David (2018), *Humanology*, Dublin: Gill.

Patterson, Charles (2002), *Eternal Treblinka: Our Treatment of Animals and the Holocaust*, Brooklyn, NY: Lantern Books.

Preciado, Paul B. (2018), *Countersexual Manifesto*, New York: Columbia University Press.

Queer Death Studies Network, https://queerdeathstudies.wordpress.com/.

Rancière, Jacques (1995), *On the Shores of Politics*, trans. Liz Heron, London: Verso.

Rancière, Jacques (2007), *The Future of the Image*, trans. Gregory Elliot, London: Verso.

Regis, Cavicula Salomonis (1995), *The Goetia: The Lesser Key of Solomon the King*, trans. Samuel Liddell MacGregor Mathers, York Beach, ME: Weiser.

Serres, Michel (1997), *Genesis*, trans. Genevieve James and James Nielson, Ann Arbor: University of Michigan Press.

Serres, Michel (2002), *The Natural Contract*, trans. Elizabeth MacArthur and William Paulson, Ann Arbor: University of Michigan Press.

Serres, Michel (2005), *The Parasite*, trans. Lawrence R. Schehr, Minneapolis: University of Minnesota Press.

Serres, Michel (2006), 'Revisiting The Natural Contract', in Arthur and MariLouise Kroker (eds), *CTheory: 1000 Days of Theory*. Available online: http://ctheory.net/ctheory_wp/revisiting-the-natural-contract/ (accessed 6 July 2019).

Serres, Michel (2014), *Times of Crisis*, trans. Anne-Marie Feenberg-Dibon, London: Bloomsbury.

Serres, Michel (2015), *Statues*, trans. Randolph Burks, London: Bloomsbury.

Shildrik, Margrit (2015), 'Living On; Not Getting Better', *Feminist Review*, 111: 10–24.

Simon (1977), *The Necronomicon*, New York: Avon Books.

Solanas, Valerie (2013), *The S.C.U.M. Manifesto*, Chico, CA: AK Press.

Spare, Austin Osman (2001), *Ethos*, Thame: I-H-O House.

Spiegel, Marjorie (1997), *The Dreaded Comparison: Human and Animal Slavery*, London: Mirror Books.

Spinoza, Baruch (1957), *The Road to Inner Freedom*, trans. Dagobert D. Runes, New York: Philosophical Library.

Stiegler, Bernard (2018), *The Neganthropocene*, trans. Daniel Ross, London: Open Humanities Press.

Stirling, John (1954), *The Bible King James Version*, Oxford: Oxford University Press.

Tonnessen, Morten, and Beever, Jonathan (2015), 'Beyond Sentience: Bioscience as Foundation for Animal and Environmental Ethics', in Elisa Aaltola and John Hadley (eds), *Animal Ethics and Philosophy: Questioning the Orthodoxy*, 47–62, London: Rowman & Littlefield.

Vegan Sidekick, http:vegansidekick.com/.

Voluntary Human Extinction Movement, http://www.vhemt.org/.

Watts, Jonathan (2018), 'We Have 12 Years to Limit Climate Change Catastrophe, Warns UN', *The Guardian*, 8 October. Available online: https://www.theguardian.com/environment/2018/oct/08/

global-warming-must-not-exceed-15c-warns-landmark-un-report (accessed 6 July 2019).

Weisberg, Zipporah (2015), 'Animal Agency: What Is It, What Isn't It and How Can It Be Realised?' in Elisa Aaltola and John Hadley (eds), *Animal Ethics and Philosophy: Questioning the Orthodoxy*, 63–80, London: Rowman & Littlefield.

Wewer, Elena (2018), 'Man, Animal, Other: The Intersections of Racism, Speciesism and Problematic Recognition within Indigenous Australia', *Emerging Scholars in Australian Indigenous Studies*, 2–3 (1): 24–31.

Wollstonecraft, Mary (1975), *Vindication of the Rights of Women*, London: Penguin.

Woolsten, Chris (2018), 'She sees Dead Bodies: An Interview with Ellen Stroud', *Knowable*, 30 October. Available online: https://www.knowablemagazine. org/article/society/2018/she-sees-dead-bodies?fbclid=IwAR3BbZ6b3d-IUE FM0euUScZnwwodFLNcMNxKRq9NoBHBz5fusHlyetkbKGg (accessed 6 July 2019).

Worms, Frederic (2015), 'What is Vital?' in Miguel De Beistegui, Giuseppe Bianco and Marjorie Gracieuse (eds), *The Care of Life: Transdisciplinary Perspectives in Bioethics and Biopolitics*, 47–60, London: Rowman & Littlefield.

Wright, Laura and Adams, Carol J. (2015), *The Vegan Project*, Athens: University of Georgia Press.

INDEX